TRANNY TALES

Book One of The Tranny Tales Trilogy

by LJ Chang

Published by MxTheMovement®

Tranny Tales

This is **Book One** of *The Tranny Tales Trilogy*.

Cover design and interior layout by LJ Chang
Printed in the United States of America

Published by MxTheMovement®
San Diego, California (Unceded Kumeyaay lands)

For permissions, inquiries, or bulk orders, contact:
info@mxthemovement.com
www.mxthemovement.com

First Edition: 2025
ISBN: [979-8-9987822-0-6]

Image Credits
Photographs by Patricia Lee Lewis, part of the Patricia Lee Lewis Photograph Collection, University of Massachusetts Amherst Special Collections. Used under good-faith fair use.

Screenshots from *One Child Nation* (2019), directed by Nanfu Wang and Jialing Zhang. Used under the Fair Use doctrine for critical and educational purposes. All rights remain with the original copyright holders.

TABLE OF CONTENTS

TRIBUTE
ABOUT THE AUTHOR
ABOUT THE TRILOGY
ABOUT THIS BOOK
FORTHCOMING BOOKS
CONTENT WARNING

PART ONE: CREATING — FILIAL PIETY
CHAPTER 1 — TRANSMIT
CHAPTER 2 — TRANSGRESS
CHAPTER 3 — TRANSPORT
CHAPTER 4 — TRANSPIRE
CHAPTER 5 — TRANSCRIBE

TRIBUTE

this book is dedicated to my mom, Ming Chang. in my deepest gratitude, thank you for instilling light, love, and life in me. your brightness and brilliance, your humility and humor, and your strength and courage continue to breathe in my blood, my bones, and my body on earth until i have the honor of joining you, my grandparents, and our family as blessed ancestors in the spirit realm.

ABOUT THE AUTHOR

LJ Chang (he/they) is a transgender and transracial adoptee from china's one-child policy era. as an adult, he discovered that he had been human trafficked to the united states as a toddler and is a direct descendant of a modern-day slave. they were raised in extreme poverty in minneapolis (Lakota land) alongside his three siblings, LJ forged a path of self-discovery and spiritual resilience.

LJ is a multidisciplinary artist and storyteller whose creative work showcases the interconnectedness of personal stories and collective histories.

they currently reside in san diego, california (Kumeyaay land), where he meditates, gardens, surfs, and plays basketball while continuing to explore intergenerational healing and happiness.

ABOUT THE TRILOGY

The Tranny Tales Trilogy is a narrative nonfiction memoir told in three books, each composed of five chapters titled with words beginning with the prefix "trans-" to reflect a full-circle journey through cycles of life, learning, and love with ancestral, inherited, and chosen family.

spanning rural china, inner-city minneapolis, and sunny san diego, the trilogy unfolds across different settings — tracing lived experiences of control shaped by shifting systems, structures, and societies.

through an evolution of unfiltered true stories, it illuminates and weaves together the complexities of earthly experiences, the fundamentals of being human, and the intersections of basic necessities from housing, food, and water to transportation and even toilets.

serving as both a vehicle and vessel, ***Tranny Tales*** bridges worlds and moves across spectrums of survival to privilege, translating radically personal and universally relatable themes across time, space, and cultures.

honoring the universal fight for freedom, ***Tranny Tales*** offers an open invitation to explore free will, free choice, and the rights to exist freely on earth — seeking solidarity across borders, bridges, and belonging.

ABOUT THIS BOOK

BOOK ONE of *The Tranny Tales Trilogy.* CREATING — FILIAL PIETY

laying the foundation, the author explores his roots as a direct descendant of a modern-day slave. framed through the perspective of an empty glass, this volume examines his mom and grandparents' lives under authoritarian rule in rural china — during a period when communist state control shaped political structures, interpersonal relationships, and entire communities. honoring his ancestors, he embraces this sacred role of being a memory keeper.

CHAPTERS INCLUDED:

- CHAPTER 1 — TRANSMIT
- CHAPTER 2 — TRANSGRESS
- CHAPTER 3 — TRANSPORT
- CHAPTER 4 — TRANSPIRE
- CHAPTER 5 — TRANSCRIBE

FORTHCOMING BOOKS

The Tranny Tales Trilogy will continue through two future books:

BOOK TWO of *The Tranny Tales Trilogy.* TEACHING — AMERICAN DREAM

the second volume shifts to the author's human trafficking and humble upbringing in inner-city minneapolis. set against the backdrop of a society that promises freedom and democracy but delivers conditionally, he was raised in extreme poverty on $12,000 alongside his three siblings.

through the lens of a glass half-full or half-empty, they recount patterns, powers, and privileges of abuse behind closed doors under the authority of a single white legal guardian. from bitter winters to periods of houselessness, this volume chronicles evolving identity and community while fighting on the frontlines of racial justice protests for Black and Indigenous lives.

CHAPTERS INCLUDED:

- CHAPTER 6 — TRANSFER
- CHAPTER 7 — TRANSPLANT
- CHAPTER 8 — TRANSACT
- CHAPTER 9 — TRANSRACIAL
- CHAPTER 10 — TRANSFORM

BOOK THREE of *The Tranny Tales Trilogy.*
HEALING — MEMORY KEEPER

set in sunny san diego and grounded in the present moment, the final book of the trilogy showcases intergenerational healing and happiness living the sacred spiritual role of being a transgender human.

yet even as the author reaches personal freedoms and pours into community from a full-glass, they confront the raw realities of a world where policies and people revert to cycles of control and fear during an era of fascism, anti-immigrant legislation, and escalating attacks on human rights.

the volume brings the trilogy to a full-circle, honoring the role of both memory keeper and culture keeper.

CHAPTERS INCLUDED:

- CHAPTER 11 — TRANSGENDER
- CHAPTER 12 — TRANSITION
- CHAPTER 13 — TRANSLATE
- CHAPTER 14 — TRANSMUTE
- CHAPTER 15 — TRANSCEND

CONTENT WARNING

The Tranny Tales Trilogy is not light reading.

before you begin these books, please know that this memoir, the chapters, and the pages to follow hold true accounts of human suffering in many forms, including: state-sanctioned violence, police brutality, slavery, forced labor, human trafficking, starvation, sexual abuse, abortion, death, racism, transphobia, adoption, poverty, and generational trauma inflicted by systems that are designed to destroy stories and erase people like me that continue to operate today.

these are not easy experiences, but they are real. readers are encouraged to engage at their own pace with care and respect throughout this journey.

13 *Tranny Tales*

CREATING — FILIAL PIETY

the moral, ethical, and spiritual duty to honor and uphold respect, remembrance, and reverence for one's family. rooted in confucian and daoist philosophies, ***FILIAL PIETY*** reflects a deep sense of individual responsibility and gratitude for previous generations, parents, or elders. it is a celebration of intergenerational connection and collective lineage — a living bridge between the past, present, and future — as much as it is an acknowledgement of the sacrifices and debts carried by those who came before us.

CHAPTER ONE
TRANSMIT

the act of passing something from one person, place, or generation to another. ***TRANSMIT*** encompasses the inheritances we carry from our direct lineage and from being born into a body on earth. the transmissions of who we come from with the emotional, psychological, material, and spiritual elements passed down through biological bloodlines — and the where we come from with accumulated histories of land, the collective wounds of humanity, and the unaddressed wrongs of the many who have inhabited earth before us.

to know oneself, we must know who we come from and where we come from.

my blessed ancestors come to me in my dreams; they call out for me to come to them. they speak to me with our stories and they surround me with our memories.

they unfurl the scrolls before me, their edges weathered, the red wax seal still intact. inscriptions from the emperor glimmer in ink, glowing as if the characters are alive with requests of responsibility.

i hear the echo of clanking swords, a metallic rhythm that dances through the air — the sound of warriors sharpening their blades, preparing to defend what we hold sacred.

the scent of firecrackers fills my lungs, smoky and electric, bursting with the same energy that fuels the lion dancers leaping through the streets in celebration of the new year — honoring us, remembering us.

i taste the tea — floral with a whisper of bitterness — brewed with intention during ceremonies, where our elders gathered to speak truth, settle conflicts, and restore harmony.

my fingertips graze the manes of the horses we once rode, strong and restless under the weight of armor, their breath hot against my palm as if they, too, remember me.

my blessed ancestors show me all this; they illuminate the way for me to recall and remember. they guide me gently to our roots so that i can feel the rising temperatures of the earth beneath my feet. the sacred soil

of the stories we must swear to share. and they come to tell me it is time to tell our messages from back in the day.

the most prominent and prestigious legacy of my lineage belongs to zhāng qiān 张骞 — an honored ancestor whose spirit calls for curiosity and courage.

riding on horseback and guided by the open skies, he ventured freely beyond the familiar frontiers of the time — gallivanting and galloping across deserts, scaling mountains, and fording rivers to discover new peoples, to listen, to learn, and to live beyond borders. he was a bold explorer and visionary diplomat that dared to reach across distances to connect.

through his journeys, he spent more than thirteen years in captivity, enduring disappointment and disgrace. yet even after years of confinement, he escaped and returned with new seeds, new technologies, and new ways of understanding humanity. he forged the earliest foundations of the silk road — a route not merely for goods, but a travel guide for exchanging ideas, stories, and shared dreams across other worlds.

at the end of his life on earth, he was recognized for his contributions with the post of grand messenger (dà xíng lìng, 大行令), one of the nine highest ministerial ranks within the government. his journeys had been long and often lonely, but he died with great honors bestowed upon him by the emperor.

as a testament to the richness of human connection flowing across continents, his spirit paved the way for my ancestors to live with courage and respect.

and for generations, we did. we were once scholars and we were once warriors — known for our

intellect, our leadership, and our loyalty. we were entrusted with guiding communities, managing resources, and advising emperors during times of both prosperity and peril. we belonged in scholarly chambers, shaping philosophical thought; we belonged walking the halls of greatness, upholding principles of purpose in every step.

for centuries until another of my ancestors took their place atop the great wall to defend against the mongol invasions. a sentinel of the ming dynasty, they stood in strength patrolling the emperor's palace on the hill. they attended tea ceremonies, where decisions were made and dynasties shaped. they participated in the royal lion dances, each step a celebration of spiritual strength and ancestral protection.

my family has carried our surname with honor. we embodied the ideals of service, duty, and integrity with an unwavering commitment to the greater good. our contributions woven into the fabric of history, helped shape the cultural, philosophical, and political landscapes carrying our people and the spirit of shared humanity forward through times of change.

the emblem of the dragon runs through my family and my bloodline, a symbol of our house banners and marking our scrolls, our stories, and our swords for generations. the dragon has served as our eternal protector — a strong yet sensitive guardian offering its spiritual guidance and blessings to my family.

the dragon is known to be connected to the element of water — the strongest and most powerful element. ruling over storms, rain, and the oceans themselves, water nourishes the earth, births life, and sustains all living beings, yet it wields the power to erase everything in its path without mercy. the dragon's connection to water reflects this delicate balance of infinite strength and the immense duality of creation and destruction — a fragile cusp between vitality and devastation.

water flows with a demure yet commanding presence. its strength lies in its adaptability, shaping itself into any form, carving mountains, and smoothing stones over the course of time. holding the capacity to obliterate entire landscapes in a single instant, water's power is absolute — a force to be revered, respected, and never underestimated.

water mirrors cycles of life and death, serving as a reminder that all spirits, once their time on earth is complete, return to the ocean. and the ocean becomes both a resting place and a source of renewal, where spirits merge with the endless, their essence flowing with the tides and storms of the world.

the dragon not only embodies power, strength, and resilience but also symbolizes the eternal cycle of existence and journey of the spirit — rising, falling, and returning to the waters that birthed life itself. the dragon stands as both a reflection and representation of the power, the courage, and the strength that my ancestors embodied during the dynasties, a symbol of resilience against the currents of time.

but even noble family roots cannot shield one from changing tides. change is inevitable and imminent, a fateful force that spares no one in its wake. as tides shift and waves recede, what remains are the stories swept out to sea that have begun to wash ashore. the ocean serving as the ultimate source of life and the vast archive of its infinite stories.

as immortal spirits reincarnating, we are tempted to succumb to the burdens, the borders, and the baggage of earthly experiences and human existences.

we inhabit the planet although we do not inherit equal opportunity to live freely.

so earth becomes a battleground once again.

and not all who fight do so for freedom.

many fight for land.

many fight for resources.

many fight for most materials.

many fight for messages of money.

regardless of reasons, every fight always comes at a cost.

who fights for the people? who fights for the planet? and who fights for profit and power?

a land rich and abundant in soil and soul cannot escape the gaze of others who covet control.

and in the battles that follow, it is not always clear who fights for freedom — and who fights to front.

wherever there is land, there are those who seek to claim it.

wherever there is life, there are those who seek to colonize it.

and wherever there is love, there are those who seek to curtail it.

in every crisis across cultures or continents, there is a choreographed chaos.

some people sense the tension building earlier than others. some may notice the subtle signs — a shift in temperature or tone, a seemingly small signal that doesn't sit right. warnings don't arrive all at once or at the same time for everyone. and often, the storm has already begun overhead before anyone even realizes to look up.

when people feel threatened, we seek shelter. we seek safety. and sometimes, we seek the stability of sameness. many will turn to comfort and others will turn to control.

there will always be sides to the struggles. they will name them left or right. right and wrong. fingers will point from this to that. there will be tug of wars with us versus them. within the groups and the outsiders too. and even the battles between. there will be community turf wars and the ripple effects outwards that entice neighbors to move with the mantra of mine versus yours.

lines will be demanded and drawn. but rarely do those labels and lines reflect the wholeness of a single life, one human with multitudes of conflicting wants, shifting needs, fluctuating thoughts, and impossible decisions.

it is those that are already armed and dangerous, wielding weapons and words, and hungriest to take the helm that are most desperate to move first.

across lifetimes, legacies, and lineages, my blessed ancestors lived with principle and purpose. but even the fiercest dragons cannot tame storms that tear through mountains and oceans when the strongest tides change course. in the end, some must bow to the inevitable to survive.

when the qing dynasty fell in 1911, it marked the end of an established system more than 2,100 years strong. shaped by emperors, dynasties, and the mandates of heaven (*tiānmìng,* 天命), imperial rule had its own flaws — where the fate of the millions were concentrated in the hierarchies and the hands of a few. but it had been a structure and some sort of standard for 400 million people. and when the last empire ended, it was not freedom that followed — but fear, and even more fighting.

although china still stood, the responsibility of governing nearly a quarter of the world's population collapsed overnight, as the central government had evaporated with no replacements.

one in four people on the entire planet were left without safety reinforcements. the roof had been torn from their homes, leaving the people exposed to every coming storm. in the absence of shelter, widespread panic took hold. the scramble for protection began, as the floodgates opened and new forces rushed in to fill the void.

from every corner of the world, the competition for power and political control erupted. while china fractured from within, factions flooded city streets and

rural markets under the banners of nationalist and communist movements, both preaching peace and progress — only to swap speeches for brutal crackdowns when persuasion failed and fell flat.

storms continued to strike from all sides as betrayal kept brewing with invasions and international wars too.

villains, villagers, victims.

enemies, opponents, bystanders.

anyone and any obstacle standing in the way of more power and control became a target.

villagers were caught in the crosshairs between whichever army arrived on any given day. towns were taxed three times in a single season — once by the nationalists, once by the communists, and once by whichever army came marching through next. farm fields were salted, food supplies were stolen, and homes were lost to fires. families surrendered their soil to invaders, their silver to armies, and their children to serve as soldiers — and still it was never enough to satisfy. survival cost more with every passing year. the people gave their all and when there was nothing left to give — no more land, no more livestock, not even labor — all that remained was your life.

as collisions of control bled the people dry, ordinary families were merely floating by in the rip currents of a flood-swollen river that were unpredictable, treacherous, and deadly.

after nearly four decades of conflicts, civil wars, international invasions, and two world wars, the cost was

staggering: over 30 million deaths and more than 100 million displacements across the landscapes of china.

no soil was left untouched. no one was granted neutrality. every village, every field, every family was pulled into the tide.

and in 1949, rising from the rubble, mao zedong stepped into the spotlight and declared a new china: the people's republic.

so when he offered opportunities of land reform, dignity to the dispossessed, and a fragile promise of peace, fireworks exploded over cities. he vowed — no more invaders, no more conflicts, no more hunger.

for many, it was a time of hope.

and for a moment, the earth itself seemed to exhale — believing that, maybe, the bleeding might finally stop.

initially, families like mine had still clung to the comforts of the past and the remnants of our old lives, tucking away sentimental heirlooms in hidden chests.

propaganda banners stretched across structures, bold red characters declaring the dawn of a new era, the red paint fresh and dripping onto the cracked pavement.

by then, the streets had been emptied of open chatter. no longer filled with the calls of merchants shouting specials, or the greetings of villagers sipping tea, or the elders practicing tai chi in the mornings. words were carefully calculated in conversations as people closed their circles to friends and their doors to neighbors.

but it became clear that was still not enough.

hope was a trap as betrayal bore a familiar face. when criticism blossomed wider than anticipated during the hundred flowers campaign (*bǎihuā qífàng,* 百花齊放), mao was offended and he recoiled.

it had been distant rumors and rumblings.

but then the opposition was taken — the politicians, the critics, the other side. the ones to disagree and dissent. the ones who had spoken too loudly, the ones who had questioned too quickly, the ones who had pondered too critically or curiously. one by one.

so people no longer spoke freely, choosing silence even in their own homes. it didn't take long to learn this new normal. any doubt in the system was a threat to the collective and any individual's personal responsibility to report on behalf of the greater good.

they had come for the landowners and the business owners. they came for the teachers, the poets, and the ones who had spent their lives shaping ideas, writing books, and passing knowledge from one generation to the next — the ones who knew too much. the professors and the scholars had believed that education might protect them — that their knowledge might be essential or that they must belong in the era of progress too. and the folk artists were punished too if they refused to paint the picture of propaganda.

by the anti-rightist campaign (*fǎnyòu yùndòng,* 反右运动), it was loud and clear that one misplaced word was a death sentence.

life was no different in rural china in a small village located within tónglú xiàn (桐庐县) in hángzhōu prefecture (杭州市)in zhèjiāng province (浙江). tónglú, like many towns in southeastern china, was not spared from the tumultuous time period of turmoil in history.

my grandparents had entered into this world and landscape of loss with a backdrop of scarcity.

fear, famine, and the fine line between survival and death shaped their childhoods. food was a phantom, intangible memory. their first lessons were how to stretch grains of rice, how to recognize roots to forage, and how to remain in submissive silence in the presence of authority. their earliest memories were of empty market stalls and their neighbors disappearing overnight. children collapsed on the dirt roads, their bellies bloated. hunger was the only constant companion.

the circumstances were so desperate and dire that people turned delusional. stripped of dignity, people were so hungry they resorted to consuming nearly anything their bodies could possibly tolerate — stripped tree bark ground into a bitter paste with leaves, wild grasses, and plant roots that tore at their insides more than they nourished. and when even those options were gone and exhausted, starvation led people to the unthinkable recourse to quiet the gnawing emptiness inside. the haunting silence of hollow stomachs led some people to the unbearable with widespread reports of cannibalism and the consumption of exhumed bodies in yang jisheng's (杨继绳) book "tombstone."

while the people were scared by purges and scarred by famine, the government continued to gaslight the public with propaganda praising abundance and pledging prosperity.

the system cemented itself into the foundations, the fabric, and all facets of life. even hunger became a weapon — a deliberate mechanism of enforcement.

hunger itself was criminalized — because to admit that the people were suffering was to expose the truth. starvation was not merely a symptom of hard times, but it was a direct consequence of policy failure. and evidence of the system's failures was not tolerated.

to speak of hunger was to indict the state, to take a grain of rice without permission was treason, and to act upon the unbearable suffering was protest. all were treated the same — each a signed death decree.

when the looting starts, the shooting starts — public executions were ordered and served as warnings to the rest. the state only needed a permissible excuse to justify violence.

somehow my grandparents endured. the intimate details of suffering lingering clearly in the corners of their eyes. the silence of starvation was louder than any cries as tears of sadness mingled and mixed with the earth. the land conspiring and listening to the drowning calls of desperation, alternating between drought and deluge. turbulent temperatures, subtropical climates, and floods with heavy torrential rainfall during monsoon season destroyed what little food was left, affecting crop yields, and withering water supplies too. unyielding

starvation led many to death's door and stole spirits young and old alike.

the severe food shortages of the the great leap forward (大跃进, 1958–1962) along with the adverse natural disasters culminated in one of the most catastrophic famines in human history. the policies promised to catapult china into modernity instead sent millions to their graves killing nearly 55 million people during the great famine (1959–1961).

dragged to the verge of death, staying alive throughout their childhood and youth had always been a negotiation with suffering. and even though my grandparents survived, it meant little in the systems of struggles. in cruel irony, they were soon condemned to suffer again — spared by nature, but their fate signed and sealed by ideology.

the first time my family heard the words *counter-revolutionary* applied to us, it came in the form of a whispered warning.

"*be careful*," a childhood neighbor had murmured before stepping away, as proximity alone tainted them with guilt.

in the square, a respected elder had accidentally referred to mao zedong by his full name instead of chairman mao. the next morning, the woman's stall had been emptied and her spot taken by a younger vendor with the armband. no one dared to ask where she went.

when the broadcasts started, loudspeakers blared through the city squares and the rural villages with chairman mao and messages from his little red book (*hóng bǎoshū,* 红宝书). on an infinite loop, the metallic, robotic voice drowned out any familiarity.

and then the boots came.

the red guard (*hóng wèibīng,* 红卫兵) marched in tight formation, their steps heavy, their presence stampeding and stomping.

one by one, homes in our neighborhood were emptied. across the nation, the same scenes had repeated in rounds.

they always arrived unannounced. storming in without warning, my family was ordered to stand aside as those in uniforms moved through.

our home had survived for generations. the wooden beams bore carvings of our family name — zhāng — and honored those who had lived and died under the same roof.

on the wall, old portraits of the zhāngs that had served the emperor and fought the mongols during the invasions were ripped down, the faces smeared under the dirt of a boot.

the family seals, once used to sign important documents, pried from its case and thrown into sacks. the iron cooking pots, blackened from years of use, were deemed government property and confiscated too.

they tore through shelves, seized books, tossed delicate scrolls on the ground. the scent of ink and incense was replaced by the acrid stench of burning pages and the sound of shattered porcelain cracking against the pavement in broken shards.

cabinets were pried open, heirlooms inspected. items that held ancestral meaning — our family swords, jade jewelry passed down for generations — were snatched too.

first the valuable, then the essential, and finally, the sentimental possessions all claimed by the state.

by the time they were done, our house was unrecognizable. and on the door, pasted in dripping glue, a red poster read: **PROPERTY OF THE PARTY.**

but nothing compared to what came next.

they had come to conduct struggle sessions (pīdòu dàhuì, 批斗大会).

in the village squares, the families accused of harboring the "four olds" (*sì jiù,* 四旧*)* were dragged forward, heads bowed under heavy placards naming their crimes: *enemy of the people*, *counter-revolutionary, reactionary*, *traitor*.

by then, the books and the blackboards had already betrayed us too. the history we knew with stories of dynasties, scholars, and warriors had been replaced with only one story: the prophetic wisdom of mao and the unforgivable sins of the past. the youth and the children had already been taught and tasked to tattle — on their parents, their neighbors, their teachers.

sometimes it was a student striking a teacher. sometimes it was a friend who cast the first stone. sometimes it was a sibling denouncing their family. some did so with pride, believing they were protecting others from threats. but most did so through tears, recognizing that if they didn't admit, their own families might be next to submit.

it was all designed to be a spectacle. public performances of loyalty. proof straight from the minds and the mouths of our youth that the revolution had succeeded.

all the fists and fighting landed on flesh. the public humiliation, the brutal beatings, the torture, and sometimes — the silence of death.

although my grandparents came into existence as proud inheritors of a rich lineage, they inherited a fate they were unable to escape.

in a single generation, a brushstroke was the catalyst that catapulted all life into irreversible change. the same delicate calligraphy that once adorned centuries of honor were rewritten as crimes and an inked mark of shame. our noble name was once etched into the annals of history through stories of scholars and warriors; but now, our legacies were reduced to a relic of a feudal past, drowned beneath propaganda, new party slogans, and policy decrees that veiled an undercurrent of control and oppression.

my grandparents were born and branded into the classifications of counter-revolutionaries and enemies of the state — not for anything they had done, but simply for who they were; not because of our actions, but because of our ancestry. with a single stroke of a brush, my grandparents were stripped of individual identity and societal status. our experiences, our history, and our voices no longer mattered.

mao's china had no place for people like us. my grandparents were never meant to belong in the new china. rendered meaningless to the new regime, they were sentenced to a future not of their own choosing.

the costs of control were pricey. my grandparents were collateral damage. they were never meant to escape the fate of the fields.

my grandparents were sentenced to lifelong conscription as state-sanctioned slaves, forcibly enslaved into manual labor in the rice paddies.

it was 1977 in the small, rural village of tónglú.

a mist clung to the hills, and the wind rolled down from the mountains, whispering secrets through the bamboo forests and grazing the mirrored water of the rice fields. the scent of damp earth mingled with the faint aroma of burning wood, as smoke from a small clay stove curled into the sky above the shack.

the shack's walls made of mud and straw, patched with scraps of debris, kept the crisp chill of the torrential downpour out. inside, the flicker of a flame cast shadows across the cracked walls.

a humble setting, yet in that moment, the precipice of existence was unfolding — a new life was about to enter the world. a faint cry broke the stillness of the early dawn and with a mixture of love and sorrow, my grandma held her newborn in her arms.

the baby girl, swaddled in her arms, was named míng, 明 — made with the chinese characters for "sun" (日) on the left and "moon" (月) on the right, representing the two things that make life go around with clarity. her name means “bright” and “brilliant”. a symbol of light in the darkness and a beacon of hope.

my mom’s birth in the shack was not recorded in any official ledger. there was no help, no doctor, no anything to alleviate the pain. the painful reality that awaited. my grandparents were already enslaved by the government and my mom’s birth cemented her arrival into a life of slavery too. to the state, my mom was another body born to sustain the nation’s granaries, another heartbeat beating the engine to power the country’s economy.

in 1978, their labor helped provide the government with staggering quantities of rice — over 136,930,000 tons yet there was never formal recognition for their life of labor. and despite the abundance they produced, the rations for an average rural household that year amounted to just about 1⅔ cups of rice per day per shack. the calculation did not account for the inflated figures and failed to add the burdens that multiple enslaved families overcrowded the shacks where multiple generations were counted as a single household. my family cultivated rice and the cultural staple for communities around the world. left with a pittance, there was no feasible way to fill their own empty cup — a paradox of abundance and deprivation.

SPRING

the day's work began at exactly 5:30 a.m. — spring mornings in tónglú were damp and cool, with temperatures hovering around 15°C (59°F). my grandparents were already awake. my grandpa moved like a shadow through the narrow dirt paths, their silhouettes barely visible in the darkness leading to the fields.

the rice paddies were roughly 3 kilometers away — about an hour's walk each way barefoot. each day, their journey was the same; they knew no weekends nor holidays nor reprieve. their stomachs already empty from the thin congee they shared before leaving the shack that did little to stave off the hunger.

the journey was made in silence as my grandpa carried their tools and my grandma carried my mom on

her back — struggling to keep pace with the others. his back hunched under the bundles of tools slung over his shoulders. his silence wasn't a habit — it was a makeshift shield of carrying the crushing load of attempting to provide for the family in a world that stripped him of the possibility to do so.

as they walked, his mind wandered. my grandpa used to have dreams too — beyond just the wishful thinking of basic respects. he dreamt of being born into different circumstances. he dreamt of life outside the fields. he dreamt of the ability to flee, and he dreamt of avoiding being brought to the fields. he dreamt of discovering a means to work for the new government. he dreamt of our lineage of ancestors and their roles and responsibilities in history, thinking *how the fuck did we get here?* his grip tightening on the wooden handles of the tools slung over his shoulder. *we went from walking the halls with emperors to walking and wading in the rice fields as tools of the state.* his steps grew heavier as his thoughts spiraled. the doubts and the dreams echoed in his mind. with a deep sigh, my grandpa straightened his posture. his silence spoke volumes — my grandpa internalized his struggles, wearing his burdens as armor against a world that sought to break him. *what was there to even say?* he led the way knowing it was one of the limited ways to extend his protection for the family.

glancing back occasionally, his eyes lingered on my grandma. she was adjusting the cloth around my mom on her back. my grandma's hands, rough and calloused, were tender in their care for my mom. she tightened the cloth around my mom's small body,

humming a tune passed down through the generations — a woven melody, a lullaby of love and courage from the ancestors.

morning mist rose from the rice paddies as the faint light of dawn crept across the horizon. the fields were flooded for planting season, reflecting the vast landscape. spring rains often soaked the region, leaving the fields muddy but fertile. the seasonal rains, sometimes light and steady, other times sudden and torrential, softened the earth for planting.

with troubling emptiness, they moved with purpose and quickness once they reached the fields. my grandpa waded into the muddy water first, steering the plow with a stoicism that hid the silent anguish of a man unable to fill his family's own bowls and a man whose only choice was to look down and work within a helpless system that offered nothing in return. the simple acts — entering the water first — were the remaining choices offered as means to show protection and care for the family. despite his bent back and weathered hands, his movements were always steady. my grandpa steering and plowing the soft, soaked soil, his presence was grounding, a silent pillar in his understanding that silent submission was the choice of survival and all else led to worse outcomes.

my grandparents waded ankle-deep into the brisk, muddy water, their bodies already aching from years of labor. my grandma followed, planting each seedling after seedling by hand. the quiet strength of my grandma manifested in every deliberate movement. her eyes, tired but keen, scanned each plant with an intuition

honed by decades. she spoke sparingly, but when she did, her words carried the worries of wisdom.

despite the fatigue and responsibility of her every interaction, her every word, she kept her gaze soft and her voice steady. "*little one*," she whispered to my mom, who clung to her back, "*do you see the water sparkle? water is life and it is alive, just like you.*"

each word my grandma spoke was chosen with care, each gesture deliberate, as if she were weaving a fragile thread of hope in a world that seemed intent on unraveling it. she knew she was the channel of light for my mom, the only display of love, resilience, and hope in a life that was painted dull.

"*míng*," my grandma said as she cupped my mom's small face in her hands, her voice barely louder than a whisper. "*the rice doesn't grow because of luck. it grows because we care to the land, even when the world cares for us so little*." her words lingered in the air, heavy with meaning yet tender in delivery. they were more than an observation — they were a lesson, an inheritance of both strength and sorrow. in her humble manner, my grandma was planting more than rice; she was sowing seeds of resilience and love in my mom's heart.

to my grandma, hope wasn't a feeling; it was an act of defiance, a choice made every moment. it was in the way she carried my mom on her back, humming old songs that had traveled generations. it was in the care she took to make every meal, no matter how meager, feel like an offering. and it was in the stories she shared, taking root in core memories.

my mom, though just a child and too young to fully understand, had no choice either but to join my grandparents in the fields. her bare feet sank into the earth as her small hands mimicked the monotonous movements. she kept going, working in silence too, knowing her labor was no different from anyone else's. there was no room for play or complaint — only the unspoken understanding that survival depended on every task being done.

the air was quiet too with the occasional croak of frogs or the swish of the water. by midmorning the sun climbed higher and the air warmed to around 20°C (68°F).

my mom's curiosity unbroken even in the face of such unabated toil — noticed a tiny frog hopping near her feet and let out a giggle, as she made an attempt to catch it in a rare burst of joy. my grandma let out a faint smile but quickly hushed her. "*not here, míng*," she said gently, casting a wary glance toward the edge of the field where government officials stood with their clipboards.

my family paused briefly, sharing sips of water from a tin can and, if luck had favored them recently, a handful of foraged greens — shepherd's purse (*jìcài*, 荠菜), the first to sprout in the cool breath of early spring; delicate fiddlehead ferns (*jué cài*, 蕨菜), soft and tender, signaling spring's first thaw; bitter dandelion greens (*pú gōng yīng*, 蒲公英), their sharp flavor marking the peak of the spring's warmer days; and amaranth (xiàn cài, 苋菜) with sturdy leaves indicating the end of spring's season.

the days stretched on in relentless repetition. the promise of a single bowl of rice was distant, but the hope kept them going.

the sound of engines breaking the stillness and the silence. the boxy, utilitarian trucks rumbled down the dirt paths, kicking up dust. its military-green body looming larger than life against the rural landscape. carrying even more government officials to survey, their arrival brought immediate tension. joining the other officials standing near the edges of the fields looking for signs of inefficiency or failure. hovering over with their clipboards in hand, they spoke rarely except for barking orders in sharp voices that pierced the silence of the laborers. in the pauses, their stares were just as deafening.

my family knew better, lowering their heads with the understanding that any form of resistance was an open invitation for punishment — a mere glance in the wrong direction was cause enough for a beating and even less food rations.

by the time they walked home, dusk had settled over the hills welcoming darkness. inside the shack, my grandma lit a clay pot, boiling a single handful of rice. they ate their meager dinner — each bite a reminder of how little they had and how much they had given.

at night, my grandma pulled my mom close and whispered stories of the past. she spoke of a time when the family had gathered for festivals, when they had owned their lives, when my grandpa had spent evenings reading poetry aloud. she had to close her eyes to remember it — already, it felt like a dream.

outside, the trucks rumbling and signaling inspections. no matter the weather, all forced laborers gathered together for roll call. their departure signaled the last light and the last move. during the night, no lights were allowed and no one was allowed to move about until the day's cycle began again.

SUMMER

summers in the fields were merciless and unforgiving. with longer days and stubborn heat, the air grew thick and heavy with moisture, clinging to their clothes before the sun had even fully risen.

the distance from the shack to the fields felt even farther during these months. the rising temperatures baking the dirt beneath their bare feet. down the beaten path, my grandparents and my mom walked the same road — tools slung over their shoulders.

the government had ensured that water was abundant where it was needed for the crops — where it guaranteed rice harvests for the state. but drinking water, water for the people, was something else entirely.

the fields were flooded year-round and an ever-present water source, but the stagnant water wasn't potable or safe. it swirled with fertilizers, human feces, and fatal bacteria. oftentimes many of the enslaved

families had no choice but to use the contaminated water for washing and drinking.

water was an essential necessity and a certain risk each day. before the work in the fields began, my grandma took my mom to find water. and at times, my mom, although just a child, was sent on the long trek to fetch water alone as she was less likely to draw suspicion. some mornings, my grandma walked to the edge of the fields where the fuchun river ran wide and strong. the river belonged to the land, but the land belonged to the government, and so, by extension, so did the water. local officials dictated when and where they were allowed to collect water, ensuring that those who were deemed unproductive or disobedient were left thirsty. my grandma bent low along the riverbank, filling a clay pot with careful hands. my mom, always watching, always absorbing, squatted beside her, dipping her small fingers into the water.

"*don't drink yet, míng,*" my grandmother murmured, her voice as steady as her hands. "*we will have to boil it later.*"

but boiling required fuel, and fuel was scarce too. some days, their rationed firewood wasn't enough and they drank the water as it was, praying their bodies were strong enough to withstand any diseases or sickness lurking within. other days, the river was too dangerous. soldiers patrolled its banks, watching for those who might steal from the state. a bucket of water taken at the wrong time meant beatings — or worse.

on those days, my grandma turned instead to the communal well. a place dictated by government rations

too, where they monitored who was allowed to use wells and how much water could be taken. families lined up at the designated water well stations, those suspected of dissent, inefficiency, or disloyalty had their water access restricted. where the entire village competed against others as to who was deemed more loyal. they were given priority. families like mine waited in the back, watching the water dwindle with each passing ladle. some families stole water, filling hidden containers while risking punishment. but when the wells ran dry, when the river was out of reach, my family turned to the cosmos. during monsoon season, they left clay pots outside their shack to catch the raindrops. although rainwater was a gift, it was momentary and inconsistent — too much in one season, too little in another.

in the summertime, the fields came alive. the rice plants grew tall and vibrant, stretching out towards the sky. the beauty was deceptive though as the work became more grueling. the heat wrapped around them like a suffocating blanket. the air was thick with the mingled scents of rice paddies and sweat. the water of the fields, once cool in the early morning, turned warm and stagnant, clinging to their skin like an unwelcome second layer.

weeding the paddies meant hours spent crouching, their legs hidden, fully submerged and waist-deep in water. moving methodically, their hands tirelessly pulling up invasive grasses that threatened the crops with their survival depending on this very food.

along the neglected corners and edges of the fields, with raw and blistered hands, my grandma

reached for water spinach (*kōng xīn cài*, 空心菜) that thrived in the summer heat, its hollow stems floating above the murky water. on the luckiest days, my mom helped her dig for lotus shoots (*lián ǒu*, 莲藕) hidden beneath the mud — a small treasure of a meal. and on rare days, my grandma pulled purslane (*mǎ chǐ xiàn*, 马齿苋) — a petite plant with a tangy taste that offered little nourishment during the summer heat. the occasional breeze was a vanishing breather, carrying the earthy aroma of freshly unearthed lotus roots. my mom's hands, though small, had become deft at pulling them from the muck, her nails perpetually caked with dirt.

my mom watched her closely, through these acts of foraging and arduous labor, she digested lessons that went beyond survival — inheriting the intimate connection to the land, learning its gifts, and its daily duties. just as there was no choice in which plants the fields might offer to forage, there was no space for the luxuries of childhood lust. identity shaped in the shadows of hardship and by the necessities of survival, wonders of personality, self-discovery and freedom knew no nurture nor growth.

with a vibrant personality, my mom was a sharp contrast to the muted life she was forced to live. naturally curious, and always asking questions that my grandma answered with a faint smile. she had a playful streak too — splashing water in the paddies when no one was looking or sticking her tongue out at the reflection of an official in a muddy puddle. her moments of rebellion were subtle but indicative — a skipped step in the fields, a quiet giggle when she found a particularly

funny-shaped root while foraging. her silliness was short-lived, quickly replaced by the solemnity demanded of her. she tucked her miniscule moments of joy away, aware that it was a luxury she was not afforded to show wholly. her curiosity, her quirks, her laughter are the glimpses of personality stifled by the unrelenting demands of survival. her small acts of defiance — like hiding a single grain of rice in her pocket — are both heartbreaking and heroic. they symbolize a spirit that refused to be entirely subdued. my mom's inability to express herself is not just a tragedy — it's a reflection of the systemic erasure of individuality and the freedoms of personality.

by mid-day, the heat became oppressive turning the paddies into a shimmering haze of steam. my grandpa, his face weathered and drenched in sweat, wiped his brow with a soaked cloth. my mom was swatting at flies and mosquitoes as they buzzed around her face. there was no true rest.

the jiěfàng pái, 解放牌, trucks appeared more frequently in the summer — their name translating to "liberation" was the irony of the chinese communist party. with the intentional, deliberate branding, the vehicles became an everyday symbol to embed propaganda. the rhetoric conveying and reinforcing the narratives of the state, that any notion of freedom came from them or signaled messages of punishments.

their arrivals breaking through the stillness and shattering the fragile flow of the fields. the heavy hum of cicadas and the rustles of wading in the rice paddies paused, the land itself held its breath too. the calm before

the storm lingered broken only by the growl of the engines — an ominous warning, like the low, rolling thunder that heralds a summer storm. like the storms of summer, their presence was unpredictable — sometimes distant, sometimes sudden, and always unsettling.

the sight of the jiěfàng trucks brought my grandpa's hand instinctively to my mom's shoulder, a protective gesture as much as a warning. "*keep your head low,*" he muttered. "*eyes on the ground. we are invisible to them, and we must stay that way.*" the helplessness to shield our family from their gaze felt like a failure more cutting than hunger. my grandpa straightened his back, his face an unreadable mask. he knew better than to look the officials in the eye, but his hands trembled as he tightened his grip on the sickle.

with government officials stepping out of the trucks, an unspoken tension pressed down on everything it touched until the land succumbed too. children were hurriedly ushered out of sight and silenced. the laborers, straightened their backs and lowered their gazes, continuing on in compliance with trembling hands, wary of drawing attention. the officials moved with an air and aura of authority, their voices sharp and commanding, barking orders that sent ripples of fear and urgency through the paddies. inspecting the crops with a cold precision, their presence a reminder of the power they wielded from the land and the lives they controlled. the remaining rhythms and routines replaced by the cadence of power and the quiet submission of those trapped in its tangles.

despite their oppressive presence, sometimes the officials came and went, but always leaving behind the palpable stillness in their wake. the fields felt heavier with their departure as the land itself absorbed the fear.

my grandparents and my mom returned to work, the flow of their labor briefly interrupted but never halted. the fields were a battlefield against nature itself. insects swarmed in thick clouds, their bites leaving red, raw welts across skin. leeches clung to their legs, burrowing into tender flesh unnoticed until the sharp sting of pain broke through the exhaustion. the static mud, clung to their bodies sticking around like an unwelcome burden.

on occasions, a sudden summer storm swept in, the skies darkening as thunder rumbled in the distance. lightning splitting the horizon, and the first drops of rain were a brief reprieve from the incessant heat. but the storms often brought destruction as much as relief. torrential downpours flooding the paddies, washing away the fragile seedlings they had worked so hard to plant. my grandparents and the others scrambling to salvage and frantically secure young crops against surging water. as the storms passed and the sun returned, the labor resumed, unyielding and unending.

by the time they trudged back to the shack, the sun hung low, mirroring the heaviness in their hearts. the tools on their backs — an extension of their exhaustion grew heavier with each step. the horizon was painted with the deep oranges and purples of dusk, an ephemeral beauty that belied the weight they carried. their bodies ached, and their spirits sagged under the unrelenting

monotony of their days, where yesterday, today, and tomorrow blurred and blended into an indistinguishable continuum, much like the merging hues of the horizon.

inside the shack, my grandmother lit the clay pot once more, the faint glow of its embers casting flickering shadows on the cracked walls. they shared a meager meal of the boiled foraged greens and a single bowl of rice. the hollow stems of the tender water spinach mirroring the emptiness in their stomachs and the short-lived attempts to fill the void. the boiled leaves wilting into a dark heap seemed to echo their own exhaustion and collapse.

she glanced over at my grandpa with a quiet nod, her presence a silent reassurance: *we are still here.* my grandpa sat silently against the wall, his body stiff, his hands resting limp in his lap. his face illuminated by the flickering glow, his shoulders slumped with unspoken guilt. the inability to provide — each grain of rice taken by the government served as a stab to his pride, a visceral reminder of his perceived failure as a man.

"*taste it slowly,*" my grandma urged my mom, breaking her usual silence. "*even the smallest gifts deserve their moments of gratitude.*" my mom nodded, savoring each grain.

my grandma rubbed my mom's mosquito-bitten legs, her touch soothing. "*do you know what i see when i look at you?*" she asked softly. my mom shook her head, her eyes wide with curiosity. "*i see a spark of light, míng. you are bright and brilliant. a fire that endures even the darkest nights.*" my mom smiled, her cheeks dimpling.

as the darkness deepened, pierced only by the occasional distant sound of a truck rolling through the village — its presence a reminder that the government's reach never stopped.

my grandparents and my mom lay quietly in the dark and their designated corner of the shack, their small bodies curled and huddled together against the bare ground.

AUTUMN

autumn marked the busiest and most demanding — harvest season was a time of urgency. fall brought cooler air, the mornings crisp with temperatures dipping to around 16°C (61°F).

with the days growing shorter and the light leaving earlier, the walk to the fields began earlier than usual — often at 4 a.m. my grandparents carried their tools on their backs and lanterns in their hands, the light bobbing along the dirt path like tiny fireflies.

the first light of day revealed the rice plants standing tall now — the sight was striking. their stalks swaying gently in the breeze, a brief moment masking the imminent taxing work required to begin the cultivation. the golden hue of the rice fields was deceptive, a reminder of abundance that was never theirs to claim.

the first step in the harvesting process was reaping, or cutting the rice plants. my grandparents used the handheld sickle, their hands slicing through the stalks close to the ground. although their movements were swift with precision, the manual method demanded significant physical labor and skill.

after cutting, bundling came next. my grandma followed him, gathering the cut stalks into small bundles. she tied each bundle securely with straw to prevent the stalks from scattering. my grandma's face betrayed no emotion as she bundled stalks of rice, the hefty bundles stolen before they could nourish their own bodies.

even my mom, though young, had her role in the harvest. she carried the smaller bundles, wincing under the strain, her body not yet hardened to the labor. the bundles were heavy for my mom's frame, and the straps of her makeshift sling bit into her shoulders, leaving marks that stung long after the work was done. she carried the bundles to the edges of the field to the designated areas where they were laid out for the drying step of the process. when my mom stumbled, my grandpa was there in an instant, lifting it from her shoulders.

my grandma noticed all with little to be said, knowing that words were little comfort to ease the reality of their assignment. she glanced at my mom, "*you're stronger than you look, little one,*" her tone bittersweet.

once the bundles were collected, they were spread out under the open sky and sun to dry. proper drying was essential to reduce moisture and prepare the

rice for threshing. it was critical to preserve the rice grains and prevent spoilage. my grandparents knew the process must be monitored closely, not only to stand guard against pests or unexpected rain that might undo their efforts but also to avoid attracting the ire of government officials.

during harvest season, new government officials arrived from other regions, their looming presence adding another layer of pressure and marking the height of state oversight. dressed in crisp uniforms standing in stark contrast to the dull, tattered rags of the slave laborers. even the sudden storms or unexpected infestations were ripe enough reasons to be labeled negligent and inefficient. their orders echoed across the fields, the government officials inspected meticulously to meet quotas and were unforgiving; any mistake or waste, even if caused by factors beyond human control, provoked harsh reprimands and severe discipline, leaving no room for error.

the drying bundles filled the air with the earthy scent of ripe rice, a small reminder of their progress in the process. the fourth step was threshing — separating the grains from the stalks. this was done manually by foot or hand treading, trampling on stalks to dislodge the grains. the repetitive pounding loosened the grains, which fell into baskets below. the sound of the flails echoed across the fields, a steady pattern that marked this stage of the harvest.

winnowing followed, a process to remove the lighter husks or chaff from the grains. my family used woven bamboo baskets or sieves to toss the threshed rice

into the air, relying on the wind and the breeze to blow the chaff away while the heavier grains fell back into the basket. this delicate step required skill and patience, as every grain was not to be wasted.

with the rituals and routines of harvest season, my grandma whispered blessings over the rice as she worked with an empty stomach.

the last step was to place the cleaned rice in sacks. as the harvest progressed, government trucks arrived daily to collect the rice. the flatbeds stood waiting to be filled, and officials continued to patrol the fields with their clipboards, inspecting and shouting orders. they enforced the calculated quotas — carefully counting every grain of rice and measuring the yields with rigor to ensure the state's demands were met.

my grandparents' hands clenched as they lifted sack after sack of rice bags to the trucks, each load felt like theft of the fruits of their labor.

the rice fields, once golden, now lay bare, their bounty surrendered to the state. even as my family labored tirelessly, the sounds of government officials celebrating in the distance were unmistakable. these celebrations marked the success of meeting quotas, a stark contrast to the exhaustion and hunger that defined the lives of the slaves who made that success possible. the tangible confrontation of the power dynamics of officials oblivious to the human cost of the harvest, reveling in the achievements they claimed as their own.

by the time my grandparents returned to the shack, darkness had fallen. that night, as they sat in the shack, my grandpa sighed. before he could even let out a

whisper, my grandma reached for his hand, her touch grounding, and interrupted his thought to say, "*we are still here.*"

the harvest was both an end and a beginning — all their days of labor, all their sacrifices — the seeds they planted in the waterlogged earth grew into the fields of rice that were to feed countless people and provided the sustenance and substance to sustain a nation. yet, beneath the surface of the thriving crops lay the unseen cost of their toil and turmoil — the aching bodies, the empty stomachs, and the broken spirits weathered by survival. my grandparents and my mom planting not only seeds, but the roots, the growth, and the foundational bedrock for which my existence rests upon.

WINTER

winter in tónglú was quiet and harsh — the average temperatures were 8.1°C (46.6°F) and the lows dropped to below freezing 0°C (32°F) in the coldest months.

as the rice fields lay barren under a blanket of frost, there was nothing remaining to forage. the paddies now stood empty, their cracked earth hardened by the frigid temperatures.

for my family, their morning treks were bitterly freezing. my grandparents layered patched clothing but the chill cut through with ease, biting into their skin as they walked the dirt paths. the cold settled deep into the land and deeper into my family's bones.

in the fields, the work never truly ended. the cycle of labor began anew even before the frost fully thawed. irrigation ditches had to be cleared of debris, tools repaired, and soil prepared for the spring planting.

even during the winter months, the government maintained its hold over the lives of forced laborers in the rural countryside. although the trucks and officials were less frequent in their visits, their presence loomed.

the government had implemented a system of "work points" in rural china, which dictated how rural laborers like my grandparents were compensated. it wasn't a wage system in any meaningful sense. instead, each laborer earned points for the tasks they completed throughout the year. the harder or longer the work, the more points they earned — but the calculations were skewed, arbitrary, and always determined by the state official in the government's favor. at the end of the harvest season, those points were converted into small payments or rations such as a single bowl of rice.

the careful and calculated design was to ensure a delicate balance and offset the exploitation of forced labor: rations were meant to keep laborers alive enough to continue sustaining agricultural production, but were denied the access to real autonomy and basic necessities as the government had no interest in providing beyond survival. the state ensured that laborers remained trapped in a cycle of obedience and oppression.

in 1978, the government reported its laborers' remuneration, which is effectively slave labor wages, was 88.26 yuan, about $57.69 USD per year, split among entire households spanning multiple families and generations.

bound to a system that reduced their lives to numbers on a balance sheet, my grandparents' entire year of backbreaking labor resulted in meager resources

and rations, insufficient to meet even the most basic needs.

the small clay stove in the shack became a symbol of their endurance, its fire an act of defiance against the cold, both literal and metaphorical. my grandma tended to it as though it were alive, her hands raw and chapped. "*we must keep it alive, it keeps us alive*" she told my mom one night, placing a small bundle of kindling in her tiny hands. "*even the smallest flame can keep the darkness away.*"

firewood and tinder was sparse and rationed by the government too. they scavenged for anything to keep the fire burning — gathering twigs, dried leaves, or even feces. each ember, a literal and metaphorical fight to hold onto warmth and life amidst the freezing cold.

my grandma, with hands always busy, weaved mats from straw, boiled leaves into broth, or stitched torn rags with thread. "*the earth gives us what we need,*" she says, turning even the most paltry foraged greens into a meal with a sense of ceremony. "*and when it doesn't, we make do.*" even in the bleakest moments, she carries the legacy of our ancestors. her whispered prayers over the rice fields are a form of resistance, a way to maintain connection to traditions the system tries to erase. "*they can take the rice,*" she says to your mom, "*but they cannot take our roots.*"

my grandma is a reservoir of warmth and wisdom. she is resourceful in ways that go beyond survival — turning scraps into sustenance, barren moments into meaningful memories. her laughter, rare but genuine, a fading light in the darkness, and her presence a subtle shield against the harshness.

on the coldest nights when the frost seeped through the air and through the patched walls, my grandpa wrapped my grandma and mom between his body, their bodies forming a cocoon of warmth. they shared stories in hushed tones, tales of ancestors who had shown courage and pride through the tests of time. my mom's eyes growing heavy, lulled by the hum of my grandpa's deep voice recounting our lineage. "*they survived,*" he would say. "*and so will we.*"

my mom had been born in the year of the fire snake — wise, resilient, and transformed by every trial. she spent her days and all her years as all the seasons in the rice fields blended together in a blur.

the rice fields were riddled with venomous snakes, slithering unseen beneath the shallow waters. their presence was unpredictable, yet a constant threat: survival was precarious. their danger moved both in the open and in the shadows.

my mom learned to watch, to listen, and to tread carefully. she understood the way they moved, how they lurked.

as more and more years in the fields passed, my mom grew older and she came to realize that not all threats were so easily seen. the snakes in the water were merely a warning, a shadow of the greater dangers that lurked elsewhere — dangers that manifested in human form, in the people around her, and in the system that

tightly coiled her life with control — striking hastily when least expected and without mercy whenever resistance was sensed. the venom of the snakes in the fields can paralyze the body, but in many ways, the poison of human oppression was far more insidious, robbing people of choices, dignity, and hope.

the government that owned her labor saw no need to educate her, and those who mistook her inability to read or write failed to see her brilliance. her wisdom was not written in books but carved into her spiritual being, shaped by endurance, by struggle, by the instinct to survive. the fields were both her battleground and her teacher, sharpening her intuitions, fortifying her spirit.

though the world sought to diminish her, she carried a fire that burned bright. it was steady and enduring, like the heat of a sun-drenched day in the paddies — a warmth that sustained and guided her, even as venomous dangers loomed at every step.

she was the fire snake in spirit — intuitive, wise, and protective, dodging the dangers of the natural world and the cruelty of the systems that bound her. my mom faced them all, and though she bore the scars of their venom, she never lost her fire.

my mom was both the light and the flame in a world of danger.

CHAPTER TWO TRANSGRESS

the act of crossing a boundary and stepping beyond the limits of humanity — even when such acts are deemed acceptable by legal, moral, social, or cultural standards. ***TRANSGRESSIONS*** extend from oppressive systems to the interpersonal level, rippling outward, inward, and in-between. they are cyclically passed down, passed around, and passed on. individuals become emboldened to inflict harm, exploit power, and enact violence — often concealed beneath the same veils of collective ideology that enabled it and where accountability is eroded or entirely evaded. and in the end, the most vulnerable are left to bear the brunt of compounding suffering.

communism shares a vision that everyone will be equal to each other. it seems super solid. on paper, the idea sounds ideal.

it begins where every person is declared exactly equal to one. each person is assigned the same value. regardless of the inputs or outputs, each human provides and possesses the exact same value. not just similar — but *precisely* the same. *identical. interchangeable.* any differences in needs, or wants, or thoughts, or desires are denied because all are equal and every person must remain equal to one in mind, body, and spirit. flattened in the name of fairness.

in order to ensure sameness and equality though, the system must determine the definition of "one" and "equality" in policy and practice. and then, it must execute to make sure everyone is actually "equal to one" according to the standards. it must continue to enforce the numerical, symbolic, and practical worth of every single person so it must oversee everything and monitor everyone.

but first, it must be in charge of collecting, confiscating, and cataloging everything — the land, the resources, the businesses, the homes — anything and all of the things that might indicate that people are different. any tangible distinction that might set people apart or make any one in particular seem different.

next, it must create policies and practices where people's experiences of reality are equal. where society mirrors equality in words, thoughts, and actions. and where there is no identity beyond one. the system cannot

allow one person to think, believe, see, or even question that one other person, place, or thing is at all different than equal because it creates the doubts and mistrust of equality. and for everyone to be equal, the state must approve, validate, and affirm that each is equal.

next, the system must tell or convince people into truly believing that they are no different than one and that every one will never be any different than any one else. who someone is or might become will always be the same and exactly equal to one. any uniqueness, differentiability, preferences, interests, variations in human experiences — delineation of any memory, any identity, any ambition is not supposed to be possible since each have been equalized for the sake of sameness.

even needs are no longer personal but rather political. all personal needs become lumped together and dependent on the state to distribute and decide on behalf of the collective — what each person might require and what each person might desire. the system owns these rights to choose and since every person is exactly equal to one, it supposedly makes no difference at all.

with people that choose to speak freely or to even express wishes outside of the system's notion of equality or society's sameness, that becomes a conflict. even a single person that seeks more or less than the collective is an example of "one" feeling, being, existing differently than "one". and thus, there is no space or grace outside of "one" — to feel a fraction of individuality or a person's potential or if one dares to dream beyond "equal" and "equality".

loyalty becomes utility — the extent to which one truly believes in the idea of absolute equality determines basic human needs such as food or housing or healthcare. even these become conditional rewards or punishments dependent on one's ability to uphold the system's equality and the ideology that all are equal. those who do not believe or align or fall in line to equality are deviating outliers that feel exceptional — and they must be silenced, imprisoned, or erased over time to return to the equilibrium of everyone being equal to one.

and the system must monitor and maintain these thoughts, words, expressions, and actions of its people to guarantee there are no detractors or exceptions to equality. even a rational or well-intentioned thought, or a question stemming from curiosity, or pointing out these differences in the equal system, or simply asking for more understanding, it is all dissent and difference. so it must watch and track online and offline — conversations, phone calls, emails. it must impose very rigid restrictions on any groupthink — religion, philosophy, and organized beliefs outside of equality as the standard system. it must trace travel and the physical movements of peoples to the flow of ideas. proper identification systems, facial recognition checkpoints, security cameras — it is all required so that no insights or information can harm the ideology and system of equality. this surveillance becomes the system's standard and the status quo of keeping neighbors, family, friends, everyone in check.

human cravings for power, control, superiority, and dominance don't vanish overnight; they simply shift and manifest differently.

in theory, communism can seem ideal.

but when put into practice, communism creates the very things it claims to destroy especially because we do not operate in a vacuum or a separate container.

instead of eliminating power imbalances, communism consolidates them into decisions about value, worth, and needs. all of those choices on behalf of the collective are made at the top for every individual. and because every individual is equal to one, the system can coordinate and control the chain of command to execute their definition of "equal" and "equality".

yet, the same people that are also supposed to be equal to one have new positions and new leadership titles. and they can use these new positions to surround themselves with privilege — to live in better homes, to eat better food, to receive better healthcare. all the while, they can hide this double standard and still have the ability to call the system equal to everyone else. and thus, a ruling class emerges.

the promise of equality is conditional. based on ideological loyalty and utility. the system does not see any differences unless it is convenient for it to do so. except for when it suits the narrative that everyone is truly equal and that the collective society has reached equality. the illusion of fairness and equality becomes a means of control. speak up and get punished. ask for

more and that is disloyalty. ask for less, and the sacrifice is quietly taken without question.

education is controlled — what is taught in schools, what histories are included, what children learn about, what books teach, what access is provided for sources of knowledge — and it must all point back to the notion that one is one and every one in the collective is equal to each other.

the media must be censored — clips, footage, photos, videos all must be repurposed as propaganda. the current news, live reportings, the tv channels, the newspapers, the radio, any online platforms must all be carefully curated and crafted with a singular narrative of equality. the system decides what information and what programming to distribute or boost with campaign messaging that every one is equal to one in the collective while silencing and suppressing any foreign voices or thoughts that say otherwise.

the arts, the culture, and any forms of entertainment must provoke and cultivate thoughts that lead the viewer and the consumer to believe the idea that they are exactly equal while inhibiting any interpretations outside the boundaries of equality. the films, the music, the art must be monitored and managed if it has the ability to create an appetite for anything more than equality. cultural expression and cultural practices are either allowed or erased depending on whether or not it aligns to the ideology of equality.

and thus, the system becomes not just the absolute provider, but the ultimate gatekeeper.

the rise of authoritarian control swept through china like a storm, dismantling everything and affecting everyone it touched. the country underwent profound upheaval, shaped by deliberate and decisive policies designed to disrupt. what was once rich with ancestral wisdom, cultural memory, and intergenerational tradition was suddenly interrupted by new programming.

from 1949 onward, the chinese communist party (CCP) (*zhōngguó gòngchǎndǎng,* 中国共产党*)* took power and were driven to eliminate the past in order to sustain control of the future. the old world — where families had individual histories, identities, and independence — was incompatible with the visions of the new order.

in the early 1950s, mao zedong's reforms granted the system consolidated permission and power to restrict and restructure who was allowed to live and who deserved to even exist. with their strategic offense, families caught in between were targeted and trapped in a defensive cycle of survival.

by 1957, state-imposed forced labor practices were prevalent in china. the re-education through labor, (*láo dòng jiào yǎng,* 劳教*) or (láo dòng gǎi zào,* 劳动改造*)* systems allowed the government to detain individuals accused of minor crimes or political dissent without judicial trial, condemning them to a life of state-sanctioned slavery. it's estimated 27 million people died in the forced labor camps.

by 1958, the system owned 97% of farms, land, and resources. under government mandates with tight

regulations on food production and consumption, the agriculture sector was controlled with an iron grip and imposed impossible quotas that defied the limits of the land and the labor.

this fear was pervasive and prevailed in all corners of the country. closely monitored by all manifestations of the systems, local officials were driven to exaggerate production and inflate figures out of fear of punishment for reporting poor results. but the government expected and demanded their share of rice plus the excess surplus of grain that simply did not exist.

with the state seizing the rice harvests, my family was left behind with nothing — treated like animals, trained to submit, and conditioned to obey. poverty and scarcity were their constant companions. along with countless other families, they were abandoned to fend for themselves and face the sharp, inescapable edge of persistent hunger. they had no choice but to submit to a system that demanded their silence and suppression in order to survive. to refuse was to refuse life itself — as rations were withheld from those who did not comply and defiance was a recipe for death.

during three decades of mao's rule, from 1949 to 1976, more than 125 million people across china were directly persecuted, displaced, or imprisoned with an estimated 80 million deaths, making it one of the deadliest regimes in human history.

the tightly restrictive chinese communist system created an environment with a grim reality — dissent in any form is a direct threat to the state's system, sustainability, and stability. an expressive glance of disapproval or disgust or slip of an insult serve as grounds for the consequence of death. these perpetual cycles and installments of fear squashed and swallowed any prospects of reckoning. with such a culture of suppression, the monopoly of a single state-sanctioned narrative prevailed and stifled the choice of voice, severing the many realities of human history.

my ancestors did not have the luxuries beyond silence as a survival strategy. my family spent their days and their decades dictated by the government and defined by the tempo of tilling and tending to the land. hands hardened and rough, their backs bent and encumbered from endless labor, they worked tirelessly under unforgiving conditions knowing that every grain of rice they touched, every ounce of energy they poured into the land belonged to a government that saw their lives and labor as an expendable tool for the state. their harvest was not theirs to keep and their existence was tethered to the land, but the freedom to call their lives their own was an unattainable dream.

my grandparents and my mom confronted the rawest and roughest realities, but they survived and my existence is built upon the foundations of their survival. i am here and the least i can do to honor their resilience is share their personal stories of pain, perseverance and the

unwavering will to live with the respect to be remembered.

memory itself was wielded as a political tool — contested, controlled, and censored by a regime that feared its emancipatory power. there is danger in a single story and truth-telling. and as many truths continue to be twisted, those who dare to dissent continue to be demonized. it is through my ancestors that i find the courage it takes to resist, rebel, and revolt.

my family's experiences serve as a warning to heed caution. as my grandparents lived through the rise of authoritarianism in china, we are bearing witness to the same trajectory unfolding in the united states. the rise of trump and fascism have eroded human rights, erased histories, and excluded voices — the parallels to modern-day society are impossible to ignore.

fascism claims to be communism's polar ideological opposite — one far-left, the other far-right — but the experience of living under either system becomes eerily similar for the people. both promise a better world, but both rely on control, fear, and suppression to achieve their vision. in both systems, the government concentrates power and controls speech, media, education, and public thought. both use propaganda and scapegoats to justify. both punish people for disagreeing. dissent becomes dangerous and individual rights vanish in the name of "the greater good." whether cloaked in the language of equality or nationalism, the result is the same: one voice, one narrative, total obedience.

in communism, the offensive threat is painted as the wealthy, the intellectuals, or the independent thinkers. in fascism, the enemies are the immigrant, the minority, the political dissenter. the tactic is the same to defend from the enemy with an aggressive offensive. both systems demand loyalty or obedience, offering "safety" in exchange for silence. and when silence becomes a survival strategy, freedom ceases to exist.

this is not ancient as history repeats itself. the slogans may change. the flags may change. the faces may change. but the architecture of oppression remains the same. it begins with noble intentions and ends with negative impacts.

when any system — left, right, or otherwise — silences voices, criminalizes disagreements, attacks basic human rights and demands loyalty, we are no longer

talking about politics. and what are policies without bodies belonging to borders? power, framed as quests for progress and change come at the cost of individual identities and the freedoms of many.

titles have a tendency to define who you are before you even have the chance to decide for yourself. the system assigns your value before you have the agency to question with curiosity. placed within the predefined categories, given labels that determine your worth, your potential, your future. expected to follow the instructions, to execute the script, to function within the confines of a framework designed for you. a pre-programmed brochure, a pre-selected menu set — spoon-feeding a predetermined path with no room for deviation, no space to carve your own course.

the comfort blankets of titles and labels serve the revolving door of individual ideologies and people in positions of power and privileges. a societal title or material status are fleeting concepts that may grant a fading illusion of protection or safety, but when the façade crumbles, no one is spared. the absence of temporary titles and hierarchies reveal the raw reality of individual fights or flights to avoid who they truly are — no title can disguise one's character, one's humanity, or one's true spirit.

the elites of yesterday are not today's elite and they will not be tomorrow's, as power is transient. tides, like power, are ever-changing — ebb and flow are their nature. and when the tides shift again, as they always do, they leave no space to hide, forcing the confrontation of the human spirit with the truth that was always beneath the surface. and even the elite are not immune from the tides of time inevitably shifting, rewriting the order of the world.

still, many believe they are safe. and yet, people continue to sit on the sidelines convinced they are safe. they think if they remain quiet, it will not reach them. that comfort is immunity. that neutrality is protection. that if they stay put, none of it will touch them directly. but oppression does not stay contained in a corner. it spreads — from the margins to the mainstream. it reaches into homes, workplaces, schools, communities, families and friends. from the periphery to the heart of societies to the central thoughts of minds.

by the time it arrives at the door, it is too late to pretend it wasn't coming. those who once believed they were unaffected will find themselves asking how they didn't see the storm coming.

weaponization of fear is not a relic of the past but the timeless tool and currency of control for every authoritarian regime. whether it is mao or trump, the mechanisms of oppression remain unchanged, recycled through different faces and names. in situations of oppression, there is no passive middle ground when the tides of history are turning.

everyone is vulnerable and a target to a regime determined to erase the past and reshape the future. first, they come for the peoples and politicians opposing them. next, they come for the families with wealth — in resources, in money, in land, in knowledge, in social networks, in social capital, in influence.

relationships are the currency of powerful change, so they come for those who know too much and move too well — the ones who navigate systems successfully, the ones who organize in community symbiotically, the ones who understand how to disrupt the power plugs.

then, they come for the ones too aligned, too insulated to feel affected. then, they come for the middle that bear witness through windows and screens to the pain in plain sight. and then they must come for the intellectuals, the intuitive, and the inquisitive. for the communities in the rural outskirts, the people in the suburban neighborhoods, and the ones in the heart of the inner cities. they come for the artists, the writers, and the creatives too. they have reason to come for anyone standing in their path and the ones who know to stand together.

history tends to repeat itself in the cycles of karma and trauma until the masses have fulfilled the courage to challenge the status quo from the masters.

---

on the street with the literal meaning for eternal peace, blood from thousands of dead bodies poured onto chang'an boulevard (*cháng'ān jiē*, 长安街) and into the capital of běijīng. across china, millions of students had filled the streets and the square with poetry and protests. the masses gathered in tiān'ānmén (gate of heavenly peace) dreaming of democracy and dignity, resistance and reform.

but the tanks came rolling in and with them, they crushed and cracked down. on all those who fought on the frontlines of freedom for a better future of china in 1989.

for a brief moment, history cracked open while the eyes of the world turned to běijīng.

may 35th, VIIV, 8^2, 8964, 六四屠殺, *liù-sì túshā.*

the date remains censored and silenced.

only five photographers managed to smuggle images out of běijīng that day. hidden in boxes of tea, flushed down hotel toilets, or stuffed inside shoes. they risked everything to allow the world to watch and bear witness. the images — grainy, zoomed-in, blurred — became the most iconic photographs of the 20th century, because they were nearly the only ones that made it out.

it's not over.

not yet.

the world outside shifted and surged with its own cries of uprisings and revolution, but with hope squashed in the square, my family remained trapped in an unchanging cycle shaped by the tides of control and the silenced strength it took to endure. the fields were their battlefield, their teacher, and their prison, where my family bore the brunt of the state's cruelty.

by the sweeping changes of the up to the mountains and down to the countryside movement, (shàngshān xiàxiāng yùndòng, 上山下乡运, 1968-1978), my grandparents were already trapped in a system that never allowed them to leave. the policy sent 16 million urban youth from educated and intellectual households to the fields too. but unlike the educated city youth who were later allowed to return, my family had nowhere to return to and no escape. their fate was written into the very soil they tilled.

by 1968, my family had been subjected to forced labor, condemned to a life where escape was impossible as government surveillance tightened its grip. for nearly three decades, the rhythms and routines of my family's life in slavery remained the same, dictated by the government's demands and the unforgiving cycles of nature.

time stood quite still in the rice paddies. and so the passing years brought no changes to their days — only the relentless repetition of planting, weeding, harvesting. defined by backbreaking labor, each season unfolded with a grim predictability. for thirty years, the seasons passed in a blur of labor, each one nearly indistinguishable from the last — except for the last and final year.

as the days bled into one another, the season reached its peak during the mid-autumn moon festival (中秋, or zhōngqiū jié, 中秋节). a time meant for tradition and celebration, with centuries-old cultures and customs, to honor the crops under the glow of the full moon to symbolize its completeness and togetherness was void of its rituals and routine joys.

during harvest season, the government jiěfàng pái trucks arrived daily. each bringing new foreign faces and government officials with the same agenda: enforce the national agricultural quotas and execute the family planning policies that had gripped the nation since 1979. their visits were brief and transient. at the end of the day, the sound of their laughter and clinking of glasses drifted across the fields striking with unmistaken celebration. they came, they saw, they conquered — they arrived, they seized what they wanted, and they left for the next village.

daily arrivals came again on september 27, 1996.

the air inside the administrative hall was thick with the scent of burning opium, curling in ghostly tendrils from pipes clutched between yellowed teeth. the smell mixed with the sharp tang of báijiǔ, poured into small, delicate porcelain cups, the kind that had once graced the tables of emperors. the walls, once pristine, were stained with years of tobacco smoke and the sweat of desperate men.

at the long wooden table, two groups of men sat in uneven clusters — the rural village officials and the new arrivals of government officials. sent on behalf of the national interests, the newcomers wore their power like a polished second skin. unlike the rural village officials, their postures stiff with deference, their eyes darting anxiously for approval, these men reeked of entitlement.

the rural village chief, an aging man with hollow cheeks and the sun-weathered skin of a lifetime spent in the stress of appeasing, poured another round. the younger rural village officials followed suit, they smiled too broadly, nodded too eagerly, excited to impress but knowing their place. laughing too loudly at the jokes of the government officials, each tried to outshine the others, hoping to stand out and secure a coveted position among the new government ranks. their eyes darting anxiously between one another seeking approval and to prove their worth.

the highest-ranking official among the newcomers leaned back in his chair, exhaling a stream of

smoke from his nostrils. "*it's good,*" he mused, swirling the liquor in his cup, "*to see how hard you all work here. to see the commitment to the Party. the loyalty to the nation*" his voice was thick with amusement, patronizing, the way a master praises the particularly obedient.

the rural village officials nodded in fervent agreement.

"*we do our duty, director,*" the rural village chief said quickly, lowering his head in an exaggerated show of respect and acknowledgement that they must follow the chain of command. he shared "*the quotas have been met and the numbers are in line this season.*"

the director asserted, "*keep it up. i also hear stories. that some of you... understand certain indulgences.*" he gave a slow, subtle smile, his eyes flicking toward one of the younger rural village officers, a man who had been uncharacteristically quiet. the younger man tensed but forced a nervous laugh.

"*indulgences?*" he echoed, shifting in his seat. "*we understand your orders, director.*"

the room tensed for a moment, but then the director chuckled, slapping the table. "*don't be so stiff, we're among men here.*" he turned to the others, his eyes gleaming with amusement. "*tell me, have any been causing trouble? have they been upholding the national policies?*"

one of the younger rural village officials smirked, sipping his báijiǔ. eager to prove himself, he leaned forward and with slick flattery declared "*we ensure every family obeys the quotas and follows the*" *policy, director. no exceptions. there are always those who serve the Party loyally.*" he let the words hang, a carefully placed offering.

a few of the other rural village officials laughed. it was a game, this exchange — one where the lower men knew their role. they played along, even as they seethed in seeking out a winning stamp of approval. the officials exchanged glances before the director smirked. "*is that so?*"

a silence fell. the unspoken words thickened the air like the smoke that swirled above them. the rural village chief, emboldened, poured another round and let his voice drop into darkness.

"*there are always some…*," he said carefully, eyes flicking toward the door. "*girls whose families know to obey. if you wish, you can meet them yourself.*"

the director let out a slow, satisfied exhale, tapping ash from his pipe. "*loyalty,*" he mused, "*is best shown in action.*"

the lower men nodding, their spines bending as easily as the reeds in the fields outside. power was a currency, and in that room, they were eager to spend it freely. power was intoxicating — both in the way it coursed through their veins with each drink and in the way it allowed them to bend the fates of those beneath them without consequence.

outside, beyond the thick wooden doors of the well-guarded confines of the administrative building, the village lay silent under the exhaust of harvest season. these men were the self-proclaimed architects of the new china, indulging in the very excesses they denounced.

their rhetoric spoke of discipline, of equality, of the necessity of sacrifice, but their actions betrayed the truth — there were always those who feasted while others starved.

the government officials decided to take the jiěfàng pái trucks out for a spin that evening.

since my mom was born into slavery. as a slave, consequently there is no such thing as autonomy, no space to choose, and no say to what was forced upon her. my mom's body, like her labor, was also property of the government.

my mom was petite to say the least. small, standing nowhere near five feet tall, weighing in at 90 pounds is generous. my mom had long, beautiful black hair down to her waist that framed the delicate features in her face. she had my grandma's resilience and my grandpa's silent strength, but neither were able to defend her from the violence to come.

crawling out of the trucks and entering my family's shack, the director's presence was shrouded in authority and unchecked power. he was a man of rank, a proud symbol of the state's ultimate control. and to him, she was not a person but yet another piece of property and an extended product of his title.

his gaze lingered too long on my mom, a look heavy with keenness. as he closed the distance between them, his gait was deliberate in his approach towards my mom. with trepidation, my grandma and grandpa had already moved in between, instinctively stepping in the way in a desperate attempt to shield her.

unmoved, rather provoked and agitated further by their feeble attempt at defiance. with a forceful motion, he shoved my grandparents. he scoffed at their frail bodies stumbling, clearly they were no match. a grim foreshadowing of the violence to follow — a preview of a cruelty they were powerless to stop.

as my grandparents staggered from his shove, their breaths caught in their chests. my grandpa's calloused hands clenched into fists at his sides, trembling not from fear but from the knowledge that any resistance beyond this moment would only make things worse for all of them. my grandma, frail yet determined, grasped for my mom, her fingers brushing against the fabric of my mom's sleeve before the director's presence loomed over them all like an unmovable shadow.

he towered over my mom, whose small frame seemed to shrink under his looming presence. she stood frozen, her face pale, her hands trembling. my grandpa tried to step forward again, his voice firm as he pleaded, "*please, no stop.*"

the director ignored him with ease, his expression darkening as if his words were an affront to his authority. his hand shot out, grabbing my mom by the arm, his grip harsh enough to leave bruises. my mom was pulled forward.

he motioned to one of the other rural government officials with a curt nod. the message was clear: deal with them. the young rural government official stepped forward, his movements calculated as he stood between my grandparents and the man who now dragged my mom further away.

my grandparents cries grew louder, their voices breaking, "*míng! míng!*" my grandpa's eyes filled with helpless fury and deep sorrow, knowing any further resistance will bring death.

the director led my mom behind the shack. the sounds of the evening — the crickets chirping, the occasional rustle of leaves — fell silent in my grandparents' ears, replaced only by the dread pounding in their chests and the death in their hearts.

for my mom, the brief warmth of the moonlit evening turned to an unending darkness. the government official saw her not as a person, but as a means to assert power, to vent his own frustrations. my mom was the vulnerable target and outlet to his rage. he violated her. he raped her violently. it was brutal, dehumanizing, and inescapable.

every harsh movement, every grip of his hands, was laced with the frenzy of a man desperate to remind himself of the power he wielded. he did not care for the tears that streamed down her face or the broken sounds she made as she tried to plead for mercy. her repeated pleas dissolved into the night air, unheard by a world that had long turned its back on her.

he took no notice of her frailty, her trembling body a mere object to him. his actions were devoid of

humanity, each move a grotesque assertion of dominance, an extension of the system that enabled him, a system that saw my mom's life and labor as property to be used and discarded.

by the time he was finished, her petite frame was crumpled, her body bruised, and aching. her vision of the full moon in the night sky became blurry as she slipped into unconsciousness. the moon is usually a symbol of feminine energy, protection, and renewal, but its glow did not ease or erase the pain as it bore witness to both her suffering and her strength. the cold ground beneath her offered no solace, and the air stuck around hanging heavy with the night's occurrence.

time seemed to stretch, each second heavy with the weight of what was happening out of their sight but never out of their hearts.

my grandma rushed to my mom. kneeling by her side, her trembling hands gently cupping my mom's face. "*míng,*" she whispered, tears streaming down her weathered cheeks. "*i'm here, i'm here.*"

my grandpa stood a few paces behind, his head bowed low in the shame of his powerlessness weighing heavier than every sack of rice he had carried in his years of toil.

my grandparents held my mom tightly between them in the dark confines and corner of the shack. their hearts breaking as they knew all my mom had endured and the inevitable. my small family bore this trauma. they did what little they could to shield her, offering their strength in the form of quiet companionship and whispered reassurances. they couldn't undo the harm, but they could remind her that she was not alone.

when the director had returned, his demeanor was unchanged, as though nothing had happened. he adjusted his uniform and dusted off his sleeves as if he had merely completed another mundane task, his face devoid of remorse or recognition of the devastation he had caused. for him, it was an exercise of entitlement; for my mom, it was a moment that forever altered her existence.

he barked orders to the others to finish inspections.

the government trucks rumbled while they drank their night away and my mother bled on.

for the director, it was another day, another village, another family left broken in his wake. he didn't glance back. she didn't even know his name. he was just another nameless man, indistinguishable from the rest — he just happened to be wearing a different set of clothes in style with the new regime.

wearing his uniform — the poorly made suit of cheap material with a dumpy cut and grim color — imbued him with an inflated sense of importance. the bland cloth, designed to erase individuality and enforce conformity, paradoxically made him believe he stood apart, cloaked in authority and separated from morality. it was an everyman's uniform, unremarkable in every way, yet to him, it was the symbol of power, a tool that granted him permission to act without accountability.

the very design of the suit, intentionally devoid of expressions, was a deliberate choice meant to prioritize the collective over the individual. yet, rather

than exercise humility or humanity, he filled this void with violence. wielding his authority and leveraging the uniform as an unquestionable shield; the system granted him the powers and privileges to be untouchable, emboldening him into believing the drab of fabric absolved him from respecting basic human rights. proving time and again the timeless truth that all cops are bastards.

but no uniform, no position, no title — regardless of how "official" or mundane, no matter its color or creed or culture or country — can mask the cruelty of one's actions or hide the harm one human causes another human.

no choice. no free will. no autonomy.

it was there, in that unforgiving system, that i was conceived from a reality that is both unbearable and undeniable. understanding the truth of my brutal beginning is like standing at the edge of an abyss and there is no escaping its consequence nor any way to soften the blows.

my mom's body ached from the pain inflicted with no mercy shown. crushed under the weight of brutality and by decades of forced labor, she can still recall and recount every detail of his aggression. after the aggravated assault, there was no reprieve. my mom had to return to the rice fields, her body still reeling, her spirit forced to keep on.

the fields did not stop, and neither did the system. it demanded her labor, regardless of her wounds. it demanded her labor as it always had — indifferent to suffering.

with decades-deep aches settled into her joints, my mom was the sun that sustained me — the light that broke through the shadows of a system intent on reducing her humanity to nothing. her body was worn from years of forced labor, but she carried me. her strength and acts of defiance that rebelled and resisted a system that sought to measure her worth and value in points or rations. she was the moon that endured the darkest nights, and the sun that breathed life into existence. a celestial force that refused to be dimmed.

at the heart of the story is my mom's unrelenting courage to endure the unimaginable in the face of

dehumanization. her pain was profound, but so was her resilience. though the system sought to strip her of all choice, dignity, and respect, she found a way to preserve her humanity. she passed down strength and a spirit that refused to be extinguished. her fire is her legacy to me — her unyielding spirit lit the path for me to exist. that legacy lives in me, and by sharing her story, i honor the light she carried through the darkest of times.

the bond between a birthing parent and their child is one of the most spiritually sacred connections in existence — one that transcends language, time, and even the physical world. it is the first and most primal form of love, formed not through words or promises, but through the steady rhythm of a shared heartbeat, through the silent conversations spoken in touch, warmth, and the unyielding presence of one another.

before birth, before eyes ever meet or hands can reach, a birthing parent and baby communicate through sensation, intuition, and spiritual energy. every emotion, every whispered hope, every silent fear — these are felt, absorbed, and held within the sacred space. a birthing parent's body is the child's first home, their breath is the lullaby that lulls them to sleep, their heartbeat is the steady drum that reassures them they are not alone. the joys, the sorrows, the resilience — these are imprinted on the child's very being, shaping their existence even before they take their first breath.

for my mom, this bond was not just an instinct — it was an act of defiance, a final declaration that no system, no regime, no cruelty could sever our connection. she carried me not just in her body, but in her spirit, with every aching step through the rice fields, with every silent prayer whispered to the universe. she held me through the depths of darkness, shielding me with her will, her strength, and her dying love.

even in a world that sought to erase her choices, she carried me wholly and fully to term. and in doing so, she passed down not just life, but a legacy of love above

all else. that bond, that sacred tie, did not end with birth. it lives on in me, woven into my soul, in the way i move through the world, in the way her story breathes through mine.

to be carried in love, even in the face of suffering, is to be marked by something eternal. it is to know that even in her hardest moments, my mom was my home.

---

my mom had already experienced the heavy heartbreak of loss. the first time my mom gave birth, her child was like me — a byproduct of the same type of violence too. a small, fragile life that never took its first breath on earth. my half-sibling was stillborn, an angel baby spared from the clutches of an imminent life in slavery, escaping from the physical world and called back to the spirit realm as swiftly as they had arrived.

carrying me, my mom lived with both the memory of their loss too and defying courage through uncertainty. the laws were clear, but enforcement was inconsistent and officials wielded their power on a whim. by then, the one-child policy (*yī hái zhèngcè,* 一孩政策) had been in effect since 1979 and was deeply embedded into the fabric of the culture. the government held tight control over the lives and bodies of its people, dictating not just how they lived, but who had the right to even exist.

every day for all the months of pregnancy, my mom was haunted by fears of the unknown, knowing the only free will remaining were the questions that gnawed at her, lingering like an unshed breath at the back of her throat.

will today be the day?
will someone notice the way my body changes, the way my steps grow heavier, the way i pause to cradle my stomach when i think no one is looking?

will a fellow slave laborer, desperate to prove their
badge of loyalty in exchange for an extra portion of rice,
whisper the secret to the official?
will they tattle and report in an act of obedience and
self-preservation?
will someone's fear outweigh their humanity?
will the government find out another way?
will the absence of my angel baby grant us the fragile
protection of an only-child?
or will they still count the child i lost against me, as if
grief alone were not punishment enough?
will the family planning official see me as a criminal or
a mom?
will they come for me in the dead of night, or will they
wait until daylight?
will they make an example of me, turning my suffering
into a lesson for others?

---

my mom knew of all the consequences. she understood there was always a price to pay. she was aware of her punishment. she accepted our fate as inevitable in a system that denied control over her entire life. impending like all else, the final decision was not hers to choose. yet, in that vast known and unknown, my mom still found space for choice — the only choice left to her. she prayed that i was born a boy.

clinging to the one possibility that might spare us both. in rural villages like ours, a second child was allowed but only if the baby was born a boy. boys were seen as more valuable, as keepers of lineage and labor. if i had been born a boy, perhaps both of our existences were to be spared.

as her belly grew, so did her burden. the rice fields where she toiled had no access to toilets, to sanitation, to facilities — no respite, no rest, nor relief. with no acknowledgement of the life growing within her, her body, already small and fragile, carried me through the mud and heat, through the backbreaking labor that never ended and she worked every day until the very end. through every step weighed down by the knowledge that survival was not guaranteed — not for her, and not for me.

still she pressed on. my mom tells me how lucky i am to be alive, and she's certainly right. by all accounts, i shouldn't be here. my mom was just 20 years old when she gave birth to me. small, malnourished, and broken down in ways unseen. and yet, she carried me through it all. her courage, her strength, and her

unrelenting will to protect me prevailed as she brought me into a world that had no place or space for us.

it is because she gave me everything — all that she had — that i exist. in a final refusal to let the system strip her of the last, most precious act of autonomy she had left: giving me life.

these trials and tribulations did not define her; they shaped the love that transcends the boundaries of life and death. my mom's pain was not merely a mark of suffering — it was a testament to her eternal strength to find hope in a world that offered her none. a reminder of all that you gain from each difficult life, you gain forever as an unwavering spirit and immortal soul.

my mom was, by all means and all definitions, a slave. by deductive reasoning that makes me a direct descendant of a slave.

i was born in 1997, the year of the fire ox.

sometimes i like to think that in another multiverse my mom was a snake and i was an ox — striking a balance of coexistence in the rice paddies. the ox tilling the land and creating the conditions conducive for planting seeds while the snake controlling the pests and acting as a protector of the crops. our roles complementing each other and demonstrating a natural interconnectedness and interdependence. the ox and the snake working together in harmony to reap the fruits of their labor.

in this go around, my mom tells me that she was a nobody in their system.

but a nobody is still somebody.

and they just might be someone's everybody.

my mom was my everything.

my birth was not just an act of defiance — it was the ultimate crime against the system that owned her.

owned by the government.

abused by its officials.

as if the atrocities were not violations against basic humanity and fundamental rights.

yet, it was my birth — my very existence — that was the illegal act.

the violation that carried fatal consequences for my mom and my grandparents.

the day i entered this world was the day my mom left earth. my mom was murdered because of me.

the same government that had controlled every part of her life, that intentionally left no records of her existence, determined that my mom had outlived her usefulness.

the officials decided — *that was enough of her.*

with cold indifference, they ended my mom's life.

they didn't allow her a last word.

they didn't allow her to cradle me not once.

they didn't allow her to name me.

they took her out back, just as they had taken everything else before.

and as she clutched her beaten body, weakened from childbirth, they beat her more without hesitation. each strike was a reminder that she was never seen as a person. each blow a brutal message that she had brought this onto herself by violating the law. that she was the one to cause trouble. that her mistake went against the national policy.

when my mom could no longer fight back, when she was nothing more than bruised flesh and fading breath, they put a single bullet in her.

to them, she was always just a body, a life without value beyond the utility of her labor. her death was no different — and a final act of dehumanized dismissal, human disposal rooted in the belief that she was dispensable.

but to me, she was everything and she will always be my everything.

my grandparents had no power to stop them. even if they had tried, they would have met the same fate. and they did.

my grandparents survived famine and decades of enslaved labor. and perhaps my grandpa spoke up with one last word. perhaps my grandma had the final say for the robbery of life. but even silence granted no mercy or survival.

they were next.

my grandparents were dragged and lined up alongside my mom's lifeless body.

one.

two.

and just like that, my grandparents were gone too. with three gunshots total, my whole family was killed by the chinese government.

CHAPTER THREE
TRANSPORT

to take or carry people or goods from one place to another by means of a vehicle, aircraft, or ship. to move by force or by fate. ***TRANSPORT*** represents both the physical act of movement along with the deeper implications of severed ties. the uncertainties of the unknown and the dualities of those deemed disposable or discardable.

the government officials loaded their bodies into the truck — no words, no hesitation, no remorse.

my entire family — my grandma, my grandpa, my mom — dead and gone. their lifeless bodies were thrown into the fuchun river, discarded as waste.

my family came into this world and left it with minimal trace. my mom passing at the young age of 20, her life was short, but filled with unimaginable suffering and sacrifice. after a lifetime of survival, my grandparents met the same fate.

there was no burial, no ceremony, no honoring, and no funeral.

my mom and my grandparents' bodies, unclaimed and unhonored, decomposed into the earth they had labored on, becoming one with the land that bore witness to their pain.

in the same river that sustained the rice fields, in the same river that carried decades of their sweat and tears, now swept their bodies out to sea too. swallowed by the currents, their cries, their tears of sweat, and their seeds of suffering pooled together, conjoining and eventually flowing onward. my ancestors bodies drifting into the vast unknowns — from the fuchun river (*fù chūn jiāng,* 富春江*)* into hángzhōu bay (*hángzhōu wān,* 杭州湾*)* and finally into the east china sea (*dōng hǎi,*东海).

in death, the final traces of their existence were erased. and yet, in the unchartered waters and open territories, they were finally free. their essence becoming part of the vast cycle and circle of life.

---

there is this saying that water has memory — moving as a silent archivist. scientifically, water's structure allows it to respond to vibrations and molecular interactions, subtly reorganizing itself in ways that suggest an ability to remember the energies and substances it encounters. each molecule dances in dynamic bonds, storing the echoes of its environment, capturing the essence of where it has been and where it must go.

water is the ultimate keeper of stories, flowing through rivers and oceans, evaporating into clouds, and returning as rain — carrying with it remnants of history. it has touched ancient glaciers, carried the tears of my ancestors, and quenched the thirst of every living being. in its ceaseless cycle, water connects the past to the present, weaving a fluid narrative of life, loss, and learning. to hold water is to hold memory itself — a reflection of the infinite interplay between the earth, its inhabitants, and the cosmos.

with the empty cups my ancestors were unable to fill to nourish themselves, their unspoken grief seeped into the land. their tears of sadness and sweat bled into the same waters that had flooded the rice fields of tónglú. upon their deaths, their bodies too returned to the land.

there is no tangible evidence of my family's existence on earth. the only memory of my mom's existence lives in me, through me, and by me. i carry her presence on — her stories etched into my being. i am my mom's memory keeper.

in the same trucks that had carried generations and decades of rice sacks, transported something else alongside my family's lifeless bodies — a final loose end.

me.

they took me too.

on the route to the river, they dumped me in the street.

a naked newborn with no nothing.

no clothes, no blanket.

that was the one grace granted by the government.

to the government, leaving me in the streets was seen as the simplest solution — requiring no effort, no resources, and no accountability. the calculated omission to ensure the natural elements were to do their duty without costing the state a single ounce more of energy — efficient, consistent, and practical.

the streets, though isolating, became the indebted beginning of my story. the streets were a paradox — a place of abandonment yet also a fragile hope for survival. they offered the only chance to escape an otherwise certain death at the hands of the system that had already claimed my mom and my grandparents.

why was i spared when my family's lives had ended so decisively? perhaps it was the innocence of infancy — that i posed no imminent threat to their power, no challenge to their authority. perhaps it was yet another act of dehumanization, a choice driven by apathy rather than mercy.

in their brutal indifference, those streets inadvertently became a bridge to life, a slim chance for rescue. the juxtaposition is striking: the act of abandonment, meant to ensure my death, became the first step toward my survival.

the streets, harsh and unforgiving, carried no promise of care, but they created the possibility that someone might see me, someone might act, and someone might give me a chance.

to the government, leaving me in the streets was a final dismissal of my humanity. but to me, it became the start of a story they never intended — a story of survival, of endurance, and of hope in the face of impossible odds.

blessed are the meek, for they shall inherit the earth.

there is this fascinating notion that three generations are biologically linked to each other within the womb in one moment in time on earth. when my grandma was pregnant with my mom, my mom possessed all of the eggs she were to ever have in her lifetime and thus the egg that i developed from was already inside my grandma.

my essence, my energy, my destiny was inside, intertwined and interdependent on my mom and her mom. bonded and built as a bodily bridge long before my birth on earth. the deep interconnectedness between my grandma and my mom from root to source — with the inheritance of their experiences that lives on in my blood, my bones and my body.

as poetic as it is scientific, it highlights the profound intergenerational connection between us and our ancestors. grounded in the biology of human reproduction, it demonstrates how we are binded to each other emotionally, spiritually, and physically through the passage of time.

CHAPTER FOUR
TRANSPIRE

to come to light, unfold, or take place — often referring to events, truths, or secrets that gradually become revealed over time. ***TRANSPIRE*** speaks to a sense of inevitability of truth surfacing despite efforts to suppress. it is the unraveling of carefully controlled, coercive, and complicit realities, where the weight of consequences shift. a natural flow from obscurity to clarity with the grace and space of time. suffering cannot be concealed forever. some truths demand to be known and some realities take patience to prevail.

some days, i wish i had met my death that day too. but i suppose the details of destiny intervened against the odds.

why was i spared when my mom and my grandparents were not? why did the universe make room for me in a world that had no space for them?

a child of sacrifice, suffering, and survival.

a child whose very existence came at the ultimate cost of my own family.

before i had words or language to articulate, grief and survivor's guilt have lived in my body. permeating and following me through time, reminding me that every breath i take is one more than my family ever got to. i feel it in the moments of quiet, in the darkness, in the spaces between thoughts when the world slows down enough for the messages to come through from the corners of the subconscious mind.

ever since i was able to form my own memories, i have always had nightmares — jolted awake, drenched in sweat, heart pounding, and caught between the past and the present.

i dreamt of reaching for her. always the same, running, always running. towards her shadow through endless fields with no end in sight. she was always just ahead of me, disappearing through the tall stalks of rice. over and over, each night, i'd chase after her, my legs burning, my lungs heaving, but no matter how fast i ran, i was never able to close the distance between dreamland and the desperation of reality.

sometimes the nightmares were different. instead, i was drowning. submersed under the cold pressing in from all sides, i was searching for her beneath the water. her shadow sinking deeper. i was always kicking and thrashing, plunging and pushing to go further down. as my limbs grew heavier, i'd hold my breathe surrendering to the depths, searching for our safety only to awake gasping in the silence of the mornings.

other nights, i'd wake with a presence lingering in the air, as if my mom had been there to soothe me, just barely out of reach.

i have imagined a thousand different scenarios where she is still alive, where my family is still here. but those are the nightmares and the dreams that dissolve in the morning light, replaced by the cold reality that i am here, and they are not.

my mom had one stillborn child before me.

that singular detail altered the course of my existence in ways that are difficult to comprehend. the rationalized necessity of both recurring rape and the loss of a human baby — recorded as her "one-child" under the law — was the only conducive condition for my life to begin.

it’s a reality i struggle to grapple with, but it is the version of truth that has resulted in my existence.

outcome one: i wish my mom had never known the violation of rape, let alone twice and at the hands of government officials that left her powerless to seek justice or actionable accountability. if my mom had not been raped the first time, she wouldn’t have had to suffer the grief, the turmoil, and the loss of a stillborn angel baby. if my mom had not been raped the second time, she wouldn’t have had me and wouldn’t have been killed as a consequence for my birth.

outcome two: sometimes, i find myself wondering about a particularly selfish scenario. if the government had not counted my stillborn half-sibling as my mom’s "one child", my birth would have been recorded and recognized as her one and only child. although i would still be tethered to the same fields, confined to the same shack, and been born into slavery under the same state-sanctioned system. but we would have remained in the rice fields together, and we would have had each other.

outcome three: if i were born a boy, the laws applied to rural villages allowed families to keep a

second child as long as the child was a boy. but even then, i would have lived as she did — incessant labor without escape.

i have pondered variations and combinations of each of these options, but all lead to the same outcome as the rest of my family — a life bound by chains — chains of labor, chains of oppression, chains that left no room for choice or freedom.

outcome four: the life i am living now was the only path forward, the one destined by fate. i was born after my mom's stillborn child and that singular detail that i was not born a boy set my very existence in motion.

the irony is not lost on me. in escaping the confines of a system of slavery, i am here, i am alive, and i am very much free.

i carry with me the fire of resilience, the wisdom of my mother, and the profound understanding that everything — every heartbreak, every puzzle piece of pain, every twist of fate — happened with reason and meaning.

---

by the time i was born in 1997, china had already spent nearly two decades enforcing the one-child policy (*yī hái zhèngcè,* 一孩政策), one of the most extreme population control measures and social engineering campaigns in modern history. intended to control birth rates, allocate limited resources, and promote economic stability, the policy was officially written into the constitution in 1982, cementing its authority into the very framework of the nation as unchallengeable, unquestionable, and absolute.

the one-child policy went beyond the limits of the law — it was leveraged as a weapon of control, a tool of terror, and an entire system built to erase choice. in a collectivist culture, individual independence is irrelevant — a threat, an idea, or a glimpse of opposition to the social norms or the status quo must be suppressed. when the state decides for the citizens and the communities, there is no space for dissent and no choice

but to comply. the government was extremely strict, deploying a range of tactics, fines, economic incentives, and prescriptive propaganda. the methods used to enforce compliance became a ruthless campaign of surveillance, coercion, and brutal punishment.

local officials were handpicked from their own communities to monitor. their duty followed the chain of command and they were held accountable to evaluate compliance for all families in their neighborhoods. their performance was measured by how effectively they curbed population growth and reduced birthrates in their respective regions or assigned areas. their job security and even their own family's safety were tied to their ability to meet the government-mandated quotas. in any case where quotas were not met, officials turned to violence.

one's very own neighbors were granted the power to seal one's fate. fear turned entire communities into informant networks, where friends, coworkers, and even relatives reported violations to protect themselves from punishment. while some participated out of loyalty to the Party, most did so to avoid retribution — failure to report a pregnancy meant punishment not just for the violator, but for the informant, and their entire family.

the one-child policy dictated human worth, fracturing communities, devastating families, and ravaging generations. the message was clear:

- the future of the collective nation was more important than the autonomy of its people.
- the government new best.
- those who resisted paid the price.

each home displayed a plaque signifying their commitment to the Communist Party values, often adorned with stars indicating compliance with the one-child policy. inside, a portrait of mao hung as a symbol of loyalty.

loyalty to the state superseded loyalty to neighbors, friends, and even one's own family. compliance was not just expected — it was demanded. apathy became the currency of survival.

the government infiltrated daily life, using propaganda everywhere — painted on buildings, printed on snack boxes, stitched into textbooks, and woven into lullabies. every village had theatrical performances

promoting the policy. these reminders — painted on walls, printed on playing cards, calendars, matches, posters, and everyday household items — painted a picture that compliance was the path leading to a better life.

family planning propaganda officials — artists, opera performers, and folk musicians — traveled across china, delivering choreographed messages through traditional folk art forms. these performances broadcasted a singular narrative:

- "fewer children make for a happier life."
- "comply with the one-child policy for a prosperous future."
- "we have taken the one-child policy to heart. our lives are so great now, thanks to the Party's foresight."

even before children could speak, they were surrounded by praise for the policy. songs, TV programming, and theatrical performances reinforced the idea that compliance was the key to a hopeful future. the visuals showed smiling families with one perfect child, promising a future of prosperity if you obeyed, a future of suffering if you didn't. the state turned indoctrination into culture for 35 years.

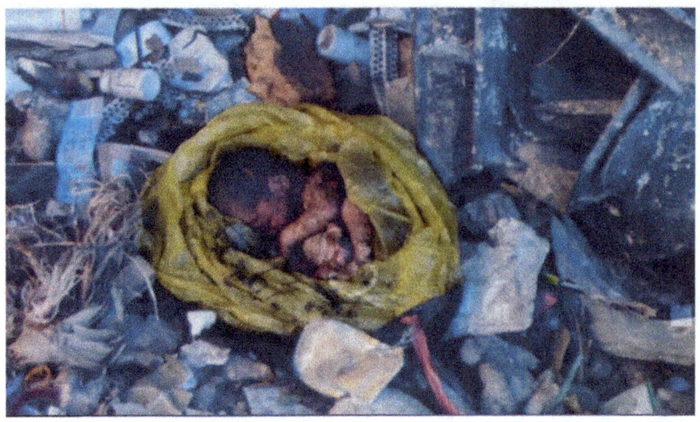

seeing babies, clinging to survival in the streets became a grim normality — byproducts of a system designed to prioritize complicit control over compassion. dissent — even in the form of compassion — was seen as a threat to the collective with consequences as severe as death.

the reality was so pervasive that it failed to stir shock or outrage. tiny human bodies, the sight of abandoned infants — wrapped in plastic bags, discarded as medical waste. dead or alive, they were left in alley ways, on roadsides, or amidst the piles of rubbish. their existence, or the utter disregard lack thereof, were indications of a system that dehumanized not only the babies, but the people forced to make such devastating decisions.

for the majority, these scenes were nothing more than part of the landscape, tragically woven into the status quo. people learned to avert their gazes, hurry their footsteps, and abide by the tacit agreement to ignore. the unspoken rules: do not see, do not question.

for most, it was easier not to see. because acknowledging suffering meant acknowledging one's own helplessness in the face of the regime.

for my mom, every path possible was as bleak as they were inevitable and all odds were stacked against her.

option one — forced sterilization:

- for people who had already given birth to one child, the government forced sterilizations.
- in those days, women were routinely abducted, tied up, and dragged by government officials for sterilization like livestock in an assembly-line fashion — subjected to forced tubal ligations or hysterectomies.
- regional teams were set up to operate with 20+ sterilizations each day. although the procedures took about 10 minutes each, they were often carried out without anesthesia and many did not survive.

option two — forced abortions:

- an abortion was a likely death sentence. rural areas were poorly equipped. hemorrhages, infections, and complications caused many more casualties.
- pregnancies were forcibly aborted. even if an abortion was mandated by the state — they were strapped down in their 8th or 9th month — their babies induced, very much alive before killed.
- it is a miracle that somehow my mom was not one of them. her body was already fragile and weakened by decades of forced labor in the rice fields. if she had been subjected to sterilization or abortion, the pain, the infections, or the medical neglect might have been fatal.

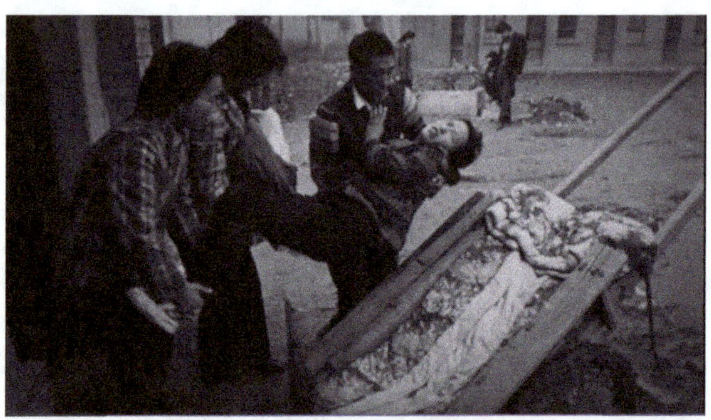

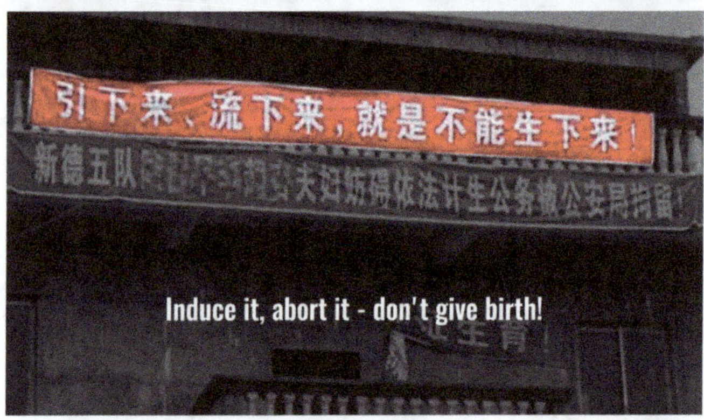
引下来、流下来，就是不能生下来！
Induce it, abort it - don't give birth!

Better to shed a river of blood than
to birth more than one child.

option three — escape:

- as a slave with no access to transportation beyond walking barefoot, my mom was trapped. and even if she had tried to run while pregnant, where was safe?
- with entire villages filled with posters, propaganda, and punishments to come for violations, escape was slim, especially given the government controlled all permits for legal travel and neighbors were incentivized to tattle.
- entire families were executed for violating birth restrictions or helping others to do so.

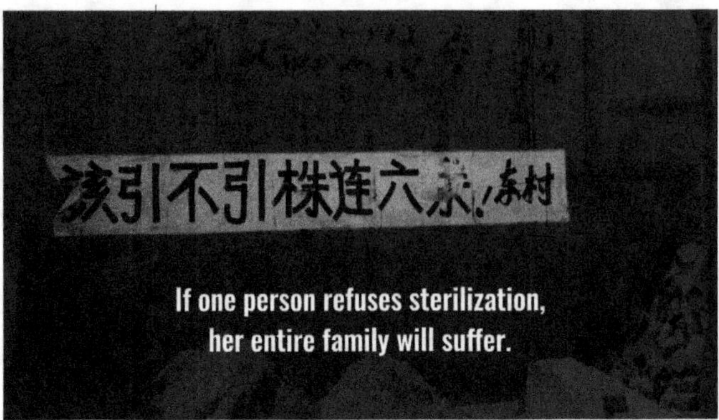

option four — resistance:

- any form of defiance or resistance — hiding, running, or seeking help — was met with absolute retribution.
- insubordination was not tolerated and the government retaliated for disobedience and any broken laws.
- homes were bulldozed. roofs were torn apart. belongings burned. often times, their lives were eliminated to ensure no party escaped unscathed.

each of these paths lead to the same outcome: my mom's death.

and yet, somehow, my mom gave birth to me.

an anomaly and an abnormality in a system designed to extinguish people like us.

yet, there were those who dared to revolt. the most radical rebellion didn't come from those with power. it came from those with nothing to lose.

the people in the lowest socioeconomic class of society — trash collectors, street sweepers, the ones the state dismissed — were the people who refused to dispose of human life and the only ones with the courage to intervene.

the paradox that the people society valued least were the only ones who valued life the most.

their actions of good trouble were rooted in moral resistance, casted their defiance to law and order.

with calloused hands and meager resources, they gathered babies others ignored and saved their lives.

the same society that deemed these workers expendable criminalized their acts of kindness, ensuring that their resistance was met with retribution. and for their efforts, they were punished. the government arrested them for human trafficking and they were ultimately jailed. but were they criminals for saving a life, no matter how small or unwanted?

for my mom, even though she had no choice to begin with, this meant that her survival depended on the silence of every single person around her. to escape notice, she had needed every single neighbor to keep her secret, to choose humanity over fear, to risk their own families' safety to protect hers. but in a system where collective punishment was swift and absolute, such loyalty was nearly impossible.

against insurmountable odds, my birth is a defiance of fate, a story that should have ended before it began. my existence stands as both a miracle and a testament to the resilience of my mom — a woman who, against all odds and expectations, delivered me into a world that tried its best to erase us both.

while people in china faced forced abortions under their government's policies, people in the united states confront restrictions to abortion — even for victims of sexual assault or incest. these realities, though distinct in their contexts, share a critical parallel: the denial of bodily autonomy. they highlight the urgent need for policies that uphold free will and free choice, ensuring that no person is forced into life-altering decisions without consent.

my mom's life — and her ultimate death — stand as a devastating impact of denying fundamental human rights. her story is one of endurance, injustice, and adversity that demands acknowledgment, not just for her sacrifices, but for the countless others whose lives were similarly erased by the system. my mom's

resilience allowed me to live and carry the call for humanity forward.

the true scope of the atrocity and the scale of the policy's brutality is staggering.

- 336 million forced abortions. for perspective, the population of the entire united states in 2022 was 333 million.
- 200 million forced sterilizations.
- there are countless generations of families whose homes were demolished or were executed entirely
- people perished from botched procedures, were driven to commit suicide, or faced government retaliation.
- newborn babies were abandoned or murdered in secrecy.
- 160,000 babies made it out of china by way of government abduction, human trafficking, and international adoption.

the chinese government claims the one-child policy prevented 400 million births. painting the picture of victory and success, they have boasted that it's made the country stronger and more prosperous, but the human cost is unquantifiable.

and then, one day, it was over.

in 2015, the government ended the one-child policy, replacing it with a new two-child policy.

with a flip of a switch, the billboards on the buildings were repainted overnight, urging families to have more kids for the future of the nation.

some truths refuse to stay buried. some stories demand to be told. no matter how deeply silenced, they will be heard.

CHAPTER FIVE
TRANSCRIBE

the act of recording, documenting information, and giving form to memory. in the context of those experiencing dehumanization, displacement, and diaspora, ***TRANSCRIBE*** represents the process of gathering scattered fragments or pieces to preserve the puzzle of personal stories and collective histories. it is confrontation of tangible truths and the creation of autonomous narratives from evidence that has been undocumented, hidden, distorted, or erased.

as a child born outside the confines of the one-child policy, my very existence went beyond the parameters of the "*hù jí*" 户籍 and "*hùkǒu bù*" 户口 systems. the nation's household registry was pivotal for citizenship, legal identity, and access to public services, education, health care, employment, and the right to marry in china.

without registration, i was considered a *hēiháizi*, a "black child, 黑孩子" — not in skin but in status. unrecognized and effectively black-listed by the state without full legal rights or protections. void of official acknowledgement, i was neither seen nor accounted for in the liminal space between existence and erasure.

to the government, i did not legally exist.

to find a baby abandoned in the street was one thing. a dead child was a tragedy, but that tragedy required no further action. it was the norm to ignore the baby and move along without consequence.

to find a baby abandoned in the street alive was another. a living, breathing infant — one not registered, and certainly not accounted for — posed a dangerous dilemma.

the state-run orphanages were not merely shelters for abandoned children; they were extensions of government control, entangled within a web of agencies that dictated the fate of those who passed through their doors. the family planning office, responsible for enforcing the one-child policy, worked alongside the civil affairs bureau, which oversaw orphanages but operated under strict governmental oversight. the public

security bureau, or police department, maintained surveillance and ensured compliance with policies at the local level, while the court system was responsible for the legal safety net to uphold the government's interests.

in theory, these agencies worked together to regulate care for abandoned children. in practice, they functioned as enforcers of state control. state-run orphanages were not always places of refuge. they were often sites of neglect, overcrowding, malnutrition, corruption, and, at times, outright abuse. resources were already scarce, and *hēiháizi* were the lowest priority, existing in legal limbo with no guaranteed protection. infants deemed unviable or inconvenient for the system were prioritized last. some institutions, complicit in government pressure, turned away children altogether to avoid the burdens.

there were no sanctioned pathways to a life worth living for a *hēiháizi*. no safe institutions to surrender them without scrutiny. no place to take them without questions. to bring an undocumented baby to the authorities was to expose yourself as a traitor to the state, inviting interrogation for breaking the law and order, and the risk of your own future.

the government did not reward this as compassion — it punished as defiance.

alone on this earth as my family had already made their journey to the spirit world, i laid in the street exposed to the elements, naked to the days and nights — a nameless and faceless baby.

yet, in the harshness of my beginnings, there is gratitude for being left in the streets — because, paradoxically, it was there that i was given my first chance at survival.

the road was both my cradle and cage — enclosing the cries that echoed into the void, unheard, or ignored. an infant too innocent to comprehend the indifference of the silence that surrounded me, as life carried on all around me.

the streets of tónglú carried a silence that stretched too thin over the unspoken — the hush of doors closing, the barely perceptible shift of curtains drawn just enough to see but not to be seen. the scent of

the river, thick with summer humidity, clung to the air, mixing with the staleness of lingering sweat, the earthy dust of well-trodden roads, and the faint metallic tang of rusted iron grates that lined the alleys.

my cries fractured the stillness. a sharp shriek, shrill.

but no one came.

the cries should have stirred reactions, should have drawn attention. but here, a crying baby was not always a call for help.

it was a test.

a spiritual test, whispered between realms, where the unseen forces of ancestors and spirits watched to see who might answer the call. did humanity still exist in the hearts of the living, or had the weight of fear and oppression hardened them beyond return? to act was to risk it all, yet to ignore was to fail the sacred duty of compassion for all life.

but it was also a test of a different kind — one imposed by the state. the government had its own ways of measuring loyalty, of right from wrong.

the wrong pair of eyes catching sight of the wrong moment might mean everything. a denunciation. a disappearance. and a punishment.

rural life in china was different. the countryside was farther from the dense urban centers where propaganda posters hung from every wall, where daily loudspeaker announcements reinforced the government's authority, and where every interaction was under the watchful eye of the state. the further from the city, the further from the reach of complete ideological control.

in the heart of china's urban cities, daily life moved in rigid, preordained routines dictated by the government too. the sight of suffering had become a constant, an unremarkable fixture of the urban scenery. officials patrolled the streets, not to assist, but to ensure that the proper order was maintained.

death was no longer an event — it existed in the shadows of alleys, on the steps of government buildings, beneath the foot traffic of hurried workers, and at the edges of overcrowded markets. there were too many. too many bodies and babies — tiny, unmoving.

to see a dead baby on the roadside was not seen as a tragedy — it was a statistic, an inevitability of the policy. those who succumbed were simply fulfilling their predetermined fate, just as those who continued to walk past them were fulfilling theirs. in the cities, anonymity was its own kind of armor — people moved through the streets unnoticed. to stop, to help was to stand out, and standing out in the wrong way meant drawing attention — a dangerous mistake in a world where every action was monitored, every behavior scrutinized for signs of dissent or weakness.

people learned to look away; they were incentivized to turn away. and as time passed, the eyes adjusted, the heart hardened, and the mind rewrote the reality of what it saw. desensitization was survival. to notice was to acknowledge. to acknowledge was to feel. and to feel was a liability in a society and culture where self-preservation depended on conformity.

in the countryside, rural china had not yet been fully conditioned to accept the sight of death as mundane. critical thinking had not been entirely suffocated — humanity had not been entirely erased. with fewer people, there were less births and babies which made each new life a bit less lost. yet the absence of dense crowds meant that every family knew one another, where every arrival and absence was observed, and secrecy was nearly impossible. the watchful eyes of a rural village served as a choice between a gift and a gamble.

the summer sun in tónglú was warm, humid — the temperature climbing above 27°C during the day. the pavement was baking by the relentless sun.

even after the sun dipped below the horizon, the night carried a damp, creeping cold that settled into the bones. another reminder that comfort did not belong either. at night, the air cooled dropping the temperatures to 19.4°C.

the night pressed on. voice strained, unraveling into a series of hiccuped whimpers before breaking apart into silence once more.

i laid where i had been left — small, unmoving, an afterthought.

i had been plucked from my mom's body and left raw, unwashed, untouched by even the smallest comfort. the scent of birth still clung to me — the sour traces of blood and sweat. i had nothing. no warmth, no trace of belonging, nothing to offer.

for 8 days and nights, my newborn body lay helpless in the street.

still no one came.

each passing hour, my statistics for survival grew slimmer. dehydration loomed with the uncompromising heat of the day. the damp chill of the nights threatened to sap the small reserves of warmth left in my tiny frame.

my existence hung by a thread, each breath a quiet defiance of the reality around me. to the world, my value was invisible, and another casualty of a system that discarded lives as easily as it controlled them. in the

streets, i existed in a state of limbo — not yet claimed by death, but not yet saved by life.

but i was never truly alone.

there is gratitude for the abundant strength in spirit, for my grandparents and my mom's protective presence, shielding me from unseen forces, refusing to let me slip into the void. there is gratitude for destiny's intervention that spared my life.

my grandparents, my mom, my blessed ancestors — no longer bound by shackles but bound to me by love not life — watched over me from above and beyond. their spirits free to roam. they used their influence to reach the heart of a stranger.

there is gratitude for the ancestors that architected the true miracle of my survival. they sent the call and a good samaritan answered our cries.

guan liling did not stop immediately. they must have passed by me every day for over a week. their gaze brushing over my fragile body in the road. cataloging my presence and learning the rhythms of travelers. perhaps they hesitated, not out of indifference, but out of caution — calculating and measuring the risks, waiting for the right moment, ensuring it was safe to take me from the streets. in a place where survival was a delicate balance, where every action carried unseen consequences, perhaps they needed time to be sure.

but on july 4, something changed. maybe it was the weight in their chest, their heart hammering too sharply against their ribs. maybe it was my uneven breaths or the way my body seemed to sink further into the abyss, a thread stretched too thin between existence and elimination.

whatever it was, that day, they turned back. and in that moment, hesitation dissolved into decision.

they reached out, lifted me from the ground. guan liling scooped me up, feeling my limp, impossibly light weight of a body that had spent too long between life and death. a heartbeat. faint. but still there.

the decision was made. and in doing so, altered the course of my life.

there was no turning back.

a person named guan liling found me on the street at the door of the silk fabric mill of tónglú county on july 4.

a feeble baby born in the rice fields of tónglú on june 26 — and on the same day, the earth inherited my

mom and grandparents. and it is through them, through my ancestors — whose bodies were decomposing into the land — that i inherited the earth as existence itself and the salvation of survival.

blessed are the meek, for they shall inherit the earth.

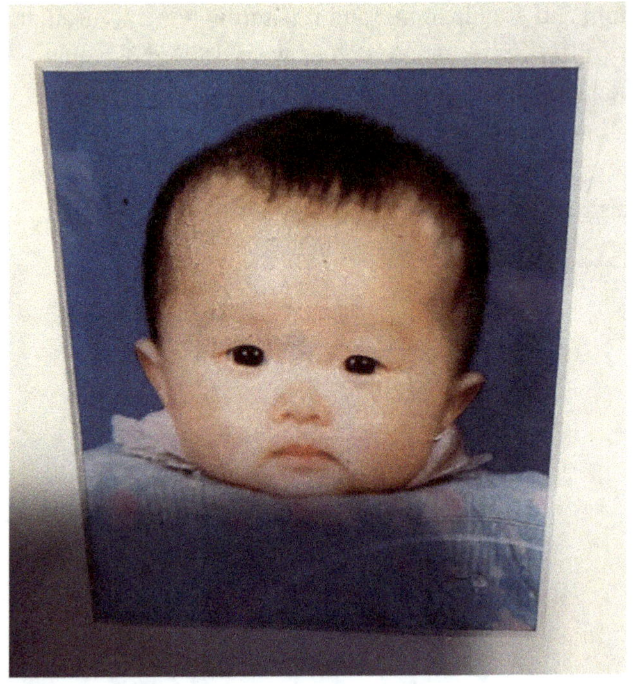

---

no longer out in the open streets, i was lifted from the ground and in the hands of guan liling.

they knew the risks. the acknowledgement of my existence was an invitation for consequence. to stop, to see, to extend care were acts of defiance.

with hurried hands, they carried me home to make their choice behind closed doors. *what now? there was no going back, only decisions to move forward.* one wrong move meant discovery and punishment. one misstep meant certain death — not just for me, but certainly for them too.

weighing the dangers, the gravity of my presence in their arms, and the impossible calculation of

choice to protect a life that was not meant to exist. for days, they harbored me in secrecy, shielded from the lurking eyes and ears eager to report and betray.

my mom says she was spiritually with them at this time. they all waited and they watched. and when the moment was right — when the path was clear — my mom led them through the quiet corners of fear, guiding, and lighting the way to safety.

on july 30, i was brought to the tónglú social welfare institute.

they gave me the nickname xiao hong, meaning "morning rainbow". they called me that because, despite everything, i was alive and i was a happy child that had the light of my mom shining within me. her spiritual presence was my lifeline — a substitute for a bottle of formula. a small token of solace in the absence of human connection through the long nights. but i had survived and i was alive.

i spent the first few years of my life at that orphanage. and when i was finally adopted as a toddler, i weighed just 17 pounds. my small body carried the weight of abandonment and the absence of nurturing nourishment. the physical marks of neglect — abscesses in my mouth — required surgery, the result of too many long nights spent relying on that bottle as my only source of comfort in a world that had not yet learned how to hold me.

the letter i was left with, though sparse and sterile, attempted to formalize the fragments of my beginnings. accounting for the date i was born, the date i was found, the date i was sent to the orphanage.

but the white blank spaces between the lines stripped the experiences of humanity and was an emptiness that paper could not hold: the grief, the emotional toll of solitude, and the enduring effects of an early environment where survival took precedence over care.

in a system that had eliminated my mom and my grandparents lives, the government tried to erase lines of my story and my existence too.

yet — here i am now. and with this very act of *transcribing* — i write myself and my family into existence — an act of defiance made possible by my blessed ancestors.

we are still here.

it's not over.

A CLOSING NOTE

this book was birthed in the rice fields where my mom and my grandparents labored and although it ends here, Book One is just the beginning.

thank you for being here with us — for reading, for remembering, and for holding reverence for my family. my blessed ancestors paved the foundation.

to be continued in Book Two of *The Tranny Tales Trilogy*...

www.ingramcontent.com/pod-product-compliance
Lightning Source LLC
Chambersburg PA
CBHW071751120626
46550CB00002B/753

* 9 7 9 8 9 9 8 7 8 2 2 0 6 *